The Boys Town Model
Safe and
Effective
Secondary
Schools

◆ Also from the Boys Town Press

Books for Professionals or Parents

Teaching Social Skills to Youth
The Well-Managed Classroom
Dangerous Kids
Treating Youth with DSM-IV Disorders: The Role of Social Skill Instruction
Building Skills in High-Risk Families: Strategies for the Home-Based Practitioner
Skills for Families, Skills for Life
Common Sense Parenting® (also in audio)
Angry Kids, Frustrated Parents
Rebuilding Children's Lives: A Blueprint for Treatment Foster Parents
Effective Skills for Child-Care Workers
Caring for Youth in Shelters
Working with Aggressive Youth
Unmasking Sexual Con Games: Helping Teens Identify Good and Bad Relationships
La Crianza Práctica de los Hijos (also in audio)
The Ongoing Journey: Awakening Spiritual Growth in At-Risk Youth

Books for Teens

A Good Friend: How to Make One, How to Be One
Who's in the Mirror? Finding the Real Me
What's Right for Me? Making Good Choices in Relationships
Unmasking Sexual Con Games: Student Guide
One to One: Personal Listening Tapes for Teens (audio)

Videos

Common Sense Parenting® *Learn-at-Home Video Kit*
Helping Your Child Succeed
Teaching Responsible Behavior
Boys Town Videos for Parents Series

For a free Boys Town Press catalog, call 1-800-282-6657.

The Boys Town National Hotline, 1-800-448-3000, is a 24-hour crisis hotline for parents and children struggling with any problem.

The Boys Town Model
Safe and Effective Secondary Schools

Editors

Jerry L. Davis, Ph.D.

Cathy S. Nelson

Elizabeth S. Gauger

Foreword by Denise B. Maybank, Ph.D.

BOYS TOWN PRESS

Boys Town, Nebraska

Safe and Effective Secondary Schools

Published by the Boys Town Press
Father Flanagan's Boys' Home
Boys Town, Nebraska 68010

Publisher's Cataloging-in-Publication
(Provided by Quality Books, Inc.)

Safe and effective secondary schools : the Boys Town
    model / editors: Jerry L. Davis, Cathy S. Nelson,
    Elizabeth S. Gauger ; foreword by Denise B.
    Maybank. -- 1st ed.
       p. cm.
       Includes bibliographical references and index.
       ISBN: 0-938510-75-4

       1. School violence--United States--Prevention.
2. Classroom management. 3. Social skills--Study
and teaching--United States. 4. School discipline
-- United States. 5. Teacher-student
relationships. I. Davis, Jerry L. II. Nelson,
Cathy S. III. Gauger, Elizabeth S.

   LB3013.3.S23 2000   371.7'82
                      QBI99-1315

10   9   8   7   6   5   4   3   2   1

Acknowledgements

We would like to thank Boys Town Executive Director Father Val J. Peter and the following Boys Town staff for their many contributions to this book: Roger Peterson, Ron Herron, Farrell Artis, Walter Powell, Michelle Hensley, Rosie Schuman, Jack Nelson, Tom Dowd, and other Education Training staff who have participated in the development and implementation of the Boys Town Education Model in cities across the country including Chicago, Dallas, and Atlanta. Thanks also to the many teachers who shared their stories with us.

Table of Contents

Foreword

School is a social experience. There are children interacting with other children, adults interacting with children, and adults interacting with other adults, and everyone brings their own background, perspectives, and understandings into the experience. Yet, we spend the least amount of the multiplied hours in schools directly addressing the skills associated with quality interactions. As we focus on the need to ensure that our schools not only accomplish their educational goals, but also are safe places for our youth, we must consider the social aspects of the school experience.

Ideally, it would be wonderful to have schools where everyone associated is able to get along, to resolve conflicts as they arise, to observe the community of learners working collaboratively in the tasks of sharing and expanding understanding at all levels. Yet, all too often there is that one glitch in the system that keeps us distant from that ideal. What are the strategies which allow us to chart that course

for the ideal? How do we ensure an environment that supports learning, cooperation, and respect?

Adults structure the environment of schools through direct organizational and policy actions that result in facility specifications, classroom structures, curriculum models, and instructional practices. Adults also provide a model for behavior which, though not necessarily recorded in any document, has as significant an impact on the environment as any stipulated policy. The divide so often evident between teachers and administrators, teachers of various disciplines, and teachers and parents is a consistent communication to the students about interactions. When we do not relate in ways that are productive, collaborative, and cooperative, we create a divided set of expectations – one set holding students to the standard of becoming positive contributing members of society and the other designed to support the territorial boundaries of individual classrooms, agendas, and concerns. We say to students, "Get along," and to adults,

"Get away." Inconsistent? Most definitely. Can we do something about it? Yes, if we own it.

At the point we take a critical look at the total picture of our schools, without shying away from the social nature of the experience, we have an opportunity to truly create safe and effective schools. The bases of the curriculum designs, the instructional and administrative systems, and the needs and nature of people all are socially influenced aspects of schools that require our direct consideration if we are to make a true difference. It is at the point of honest critique that we become able to be purposeful in our behavior of creating safe, healthful, productive learning environments.

The safe school and the effective school can be a reality only when we include the school culture in the equation. All who are a part of that school will feel there is a place for their thoughts, their beliefs, and their needs in the context of clearly communicated boundaries providing a constructive atmosphere for coming to terms with differences. That school also focuses on the importance of healthy development and learning for all who participate.

Recognizing the multidimensional nature of ensuring safe and effective schools, we must also accept the need for multifaceted approaches. When we think about the relationship issues within the school building as creating one level of concern, the possibility of needing to relate to other institutions and organizations outside the control of the school setting takes the concern to a new level. The safety and effectiveness of our schools must become everyone's concern, and we have to be ready to invite the broad participation of others with ideas and solutions which may not reside in the discipline of education. When we consider the full participation of the community – truly seeking the assistance of parents and working cooperatively with other agencies that act on behalf of children – we then empower ourselves to harness the energy of the school as a central locus of more synergistic solutions.

What are the relationships evident to students in the school building and between those in the building and those in the community? If the adults have not addressed their issues, what is the basis for the expectation that it will just automatically happen for children? We can work at strategic planning, establish comprehensive school improvement plans, and implement programs ad infinitum and still see no difference. Because we have yet to address the issue of the social relationship that is the experience in which every person related to the school participates, we do not see a desirable level of change.

The components of safe school planning all relate to people working in partnership. Whether it is the planning team coming together to determine the necessary steps, or administrators sitting down to review a site assessment, or decisions being made about what strategies to employ, it is always about people acting in concert to reach a common goal. If we take to heart the means by which the activities occur, we learn a valuable lesson in what needs to become the focus of our efforts – building relationships though partnership.

The answer is different for each school; we cannot all seek to solve the issues identified with Columbine nor any of the other sites where violence emanating from within the school was evident. We have to build the relationships with and among students that allow volatile incidents to be defused and to be used as opportunities for understanding. In one building it may be the need for better relationships between certain groups of students; in another it may be the need for more teacher attentiveness and visibility in the halls; in yet another building, the issue may be finding ways to manage the community conflict within the walls of the school. Whatever the situation, it requires an honest self-examination that explores nontraditional ways of responding to behaviors which may have become traditions in that setting.

The solution is going to take all of us working together. When we keep our focus on making a difference that matters for children, the concerns of whose problem it is, whose territory we may tread on, or who may not get a fair share pale in the interest of making that difference. The skills to get us there are ones which may be a part of a slightly different paradigm than what we have been accustomed to in education, but nevertheless, the time to make the shift is now for the benefit of the children.

This book compiles a lot of good common sense practice in one place. We believe it can serve as reinforcement for the things you have practiced over the years, for all you believe that keeps you invested in educating children, and for all those conversations with your colleagues during the moments of frustration and elation. We hope that you see yourself or your situation reflected in the stories and find a solution that works for you. We don't claim to have all the answers but we do believe the lessons we've learned over the years can make a difference for someone in a time of need. It's good practice, it's good structure, it's good relationships that make the difference, and that is what we are offering. Use the skills as a part of your larger strategy and see the difference.

As we move into the 21st century, Boys Town will continue to build on the tradition and legacy that has proven successful over the years to ensure the development of programs and services that are responsive to the needs of schools, communities, and families in the interest of providing the best care for America's youth.

DENISE B. MAYBANK, PH.D.
Director of Education Services
National Resource and Training Center
Boys Town, Nebraska

Introduction

Remember when the biggest news coming out of the school office was an announcement about the next PTA meeting? Now, it seems that school news is often bad news – the freshman who's caught with a knife in her backpack, violence in the neighborhood, or the growing list of teachers taking early retirement.

In these days when violence and frustration compete with academics for classroom time, it sometimes seems surprising that any education occurs at all. Many youngsters around the country say they feel unsafe at school because they're afraid of gangs and weapons in their buildings. Meanwhile, teachers struggle to maintain control in their classrooms so they can teach.

How can we ensure that our schools are safe and effective places for young people to learn and educators to work? Sometimes, it seems like an impossible task. However, it's heartening to know that teachers and school administrators around the country have found many creative ways to keep the trappings of a violent society out of the classroom. In addition,

they've developed successful teaching methods that keep youth engaged in the classroom.

In this book, we'll present stories that illustrate techniques for safer, more effective schools. Perhaps the ideas other teachers have developed will work in your classroom or may inspire you to develop similar techniques.

Some of the stories are graphic. Others are more subtle. All illustrate basic teaching techniques and knowledge you can use to convey important lessons to your students. The techniques and knowledge grow out of the basics of quality teaching, including building relationships with students, setting clear tolerances and expectations, and using praise and other teaching tools.

Many of the techniques described in these stories are based on principles that form the foundation of the Boys Town Education Model, a set of teaching techniques we use to teach children new skills, self-empowerment, and how to build relationships. We will discuss various aspects of the Model in a later chapter and give you practical suggestions on how to use it in your classroom.

Remember: Solutions that work for some teachers and some classrooms may not be effective for others, and you will have to analyze your situation to determine if a particular strategy or method is appropriate and safe.

At Boys Town, we've been working with at-risk youth for more than 80 years. We know all about the fears that haunt youngsters and the anxiety they live under, leaving little room for learning new things or making plans for the future. In an environment of genuine caring, we have established proven child-care technologies to teach children how to overcome their problems and change their lives for the better.

In this book, we offer that expertise to tackle the thorny issues of making schools safer and better places to learn. Hopefully, the thoughts presented here will help expand the dialogue about the importance of redefining what a safe school is – a place where students and teachers respect one another and cooperate so learning can occur, a place where open communication is a priority, a place where there is a system for resolving disputes, a place that opens its doors to the surrounding community and welcomes its residents as partners in learning. These are essentials because, for some children, school may be the only safe place.

Chapter One

Real Teachers, Real Stories

"Shut up, mother f-----!"

"You dis' me once more, man, and you're dead!"

"I'm not gonna do it, and you can't make me!"

Do these statements sound familiar? If you're a teacher in an American school these days, you probably hear declarations like these every day. They're the dangerous dialogue of a young society that seems, perhaps more than its predecessors, awash in violence and in-your-face defiance.

What's your reaction when you hear students say things like this? Are you frightened? Do you get angry? Have you stopped paying attention?

Many teachers say they have mixed feelings about school life these days. They fear and loathe the shootings and other violence that have put so many schools in the headlines recently.

But teachers also feel frustration, because they say they are powerless against youngsters who bring guns, knives, and other weapons into school buildings. Many teachers also feel equally powerless against other violent fallout – the insolence and disrespect that pervade classrooms these days. These attitudes, say teachers, are nearly as potent as the weapons and equally disruptive to the learning process.

In this chapter and later chapters in this book, we will use true stories, gathered from classrooms across America, to illustrate methods teachers use to deal with aggression and violence and make their classrooms safer and more effective. We'll show you how those methods relate to the Boys Town Teaching Model and how you can use concepts from the Model to be a more effective teacher.

In this chapter, you'll find six stories which illustrate some of the basic concepts we'll discuss in depth later, including the importance of forging relationships with your students, how to preteach skills students will need later, and what to do when a student faces a crisis.

◆ At a Crossroads

Charlie was the school's most popular senior. He had a wide, easy smile. He had letters in football, basketball, and track. Girls wanted to be seen with him, and boys wanted to be his friend. Some people thought Charlie was in a gang, but Rosalie Martin, his homeroom teacher, didn't ask.

Mrs. Martin had developed a strong relationship with Charlie. During homeroom and after school, she'd been helping him fill out applications for college. He was hoping for an athletic scholarship.

One afternoon, a student ran into Mrs. Martin's classroom and said excitedly, "Charlie's lost it. He beat up Latisha, and he's tearin' up the place."

Mrs. Martin rushed up to the library, where she found that several teachers had surrounded Charlie and were moving him toward the door. Two other teachers were huddled over Latisha, Charlie's pregnant girlfriend, who was sitting in a chair sobbing and dabbing at blood dripping from her nose.

Charlie was furious. As he struggled with his escorts to try to get free, he yelled obscenities back at Latisha. One of the aides standing nearby told Mrs. Martin that the fight started when Latisha told Charlie that he wasn't the father of her baby.

"You lyin' b----! You better watch out. Something bad might happen to you...."

Mrs. Martin had never seen Charlie so angry. She spotted the principal, Meg Dowd, at the fringe of the circle around Charlie, and when she caught up with Mrs. Dowd, Mrs. Martin asked her if they could bring Charlie to her classroom so she could talk to him and try to get him calmed down. The principal agreed.

A few minutes later, two coaches brought Charlie to Mrs. Martin's room. They told her they would wait outside the door while the teacher talked to him.

"Sit down, Charlie, and catch your breath. It's been a bad day, huh?"

"Yes, ma'am," Charlie said, fixing his gaze on the floor.

"Can you tell me what happened up there?" Mrs. Martin asked.

Charlie looked up then, and Mrs. Martin could see the cold anger in his eyes. Even though Charlie wasn't flailing his arms and cursing, as he'd been doing earlier, the teacher could tell he was just about ready to explode.

Mrs. Martin sat down across from Charlie. Sensing that their relationship was strong enough for her to reach out to him, she pulled his hands into hers. She kept her voice low. "Charlie, I want you to listen to me," she said, leaning forward slightly.

Charlie glanced up and reluctantly held her gaze.

"Thanks. Now let's sort things out here. I know you're mad. You're probably as mad as you've ever been. It's okay to be mad, because you cared about Latisha and now you feel like she betrayed you."

"Yes ma'am, I do," Charlie said softly.

"So what are you gonna do?" Mrs. Martin asked, still holding his hands in hers.

"I don't know. I can't even think right now."

"Okay, well here's a few things to keep in mind," said the teacher, her eyes fixed on Charlie's face. "I want you to think about how much you've accomplished this year and the fact that you can't get a scholarship if you don't graduate. And I want you to remember that you won't graduate if you're in jail 'cause you went out there and hurt Latisha some more. Do you get it, Charlie?"

Charlie was silent for a moment. He obviously still wanted revenge, but Mrs. Martin could tell he was at least thinking about what he'd give up if he tried to get back at Latisha. Finally, he managed to say, "I get it, Mrs. Martin. I don't like it, but I get it."

She squeezed his hands. "I know you don't like it Charlie, but you've done a good job of calming yourself down, and I can tell you understand that the price of revenge is too high. You can't afford it.

"Now, let's talk about consequences. You know that you have a price to pay for hitting Latisha just now and causing a commotion. You'll be transferred out of here for fighting. You'll have to finish the year at O'Neill," she said, referring to the district's alternative high school. "Do you think you can handle it?" The teacher let go of Charlie's hands and looked intently at the boy.

Charlie just stared straight ahead. He didn't say anything for a long time as the reality of the situation washed over him. Then, quietly, he looked at her and asked, "Can I still graduate?"

"Yes, Charlie, you can graduate. You can work with the counselor at O'Neill. His name is Mr. Moore. He'll help you coordinate your credits. It won't be easy, but I know you can do it. And you and I can still work on your college apps. I can stop by O'Neill on my way home. You have to promise me though, Charlie, that you'll call me if you feel you're going to lose your temper and want to go after Latisha. Will you do that Charlie?"

"Yes, ma'am, I promise."

Charlie kept his promise. He called Mrs. Martin a couple of times in the evening at home, but he never tried to hurt Latisha again. She dropped out of school in the spring to have her baby, a little girl. Charlie graduated with his class, and decided to go to junior college for a couple of years. The last Mrs. Martin heard, he was going to school and working part-time.

▶ **The Problem:** A troubled student needed help calming down and refocusing himself.

▶ **What the Teacher Did:** The teacher used the relationship she had established with the student to calm him, and get him to abandon his thoughts of revenge, and concentrate on what he would lose if he sought revenge. The teacher chose to try and calm the student down, rather than confront him about his fight with his girlfriend. The teacher believed that using a calming strategy would not only help Charlie, but reduce the potential for trouble at the school. She also was able to get Charlie to think about the future and focus his attention on that, rather than his current fury. Redirecting focus like this is particularly important for aggressive students, who do not have good planning skills. As part of this focus on the future, the teacher also followed up after the incident, continuing to work with Charlie on his college applications.

▶ **The Lesson:** The teacher used her relationship with Charlie to work through the crisis with him. Some of the techniques she used were: asking him to calm down, praising him when he did that, and using a steady, measured voice to remind him that he had some choices he could exercise to improve the situation. These techniques all are components of a Boys Town method called Crisis Teaching, which we will discuss in detail in Chapter 6. In a crisis such as this, the teacher must be ready to switch roles from academic instructor to counselor or mentor.

Whether you choose Crisis Teaching or another technique, you should keep in mind that some methods of intervention actually can make a bad situation worse. For example, getting yourself into an argument with an angry student won't defuse the anger; it will only escalate the situation. We will discuss intervention strategies and present more information about dealing with aggressive youngsters in later chapters.

◆ One World

In the alternative high school where she taught, Myesha Langdon had a reading class with a unique perspective – all the students were of the same race, except for one. At the beginning of the semester, the class was struggling with this.

Pam, the student who was "different," clearly was left out and ridiculed by other members of the class. And she gave back what she got by taunting the other students, calling them names and making gestures.

Miss Langdon met with Pam privately to discuss the situation. She really wanted to be part of the class and said she would do whatever the teacher thought was right to make things better for herself. Miss Langdon suggested that she use only the students' names – not any made-up monikers – when she talked to them. She tried it, and it seemed to work. The atmosphere in the classroom lightened. It seemed like the other kids were easing up on Pam.

But there was still an undercurrent of trouble. A lot of it stemmed from the fact that the students liked to tease each other by making comments about each other's mothers. Miss Langdon

had ignored it long enough and finally decided that it was getting out of hand. She gathered the whole class together, and she told them there would be no more teasing of any kind because it was destroying their ability to work together.

"We're like a family in here, and families don't belittle each other with the kind of teasing I've been hearing in here," Miss Langdon told the class. "We need to show respect for each other so we can learn together."

The teacher privately encouraged Pam to reach out to other members of the class, maybe ask them questions about what they liked to do after school, do what she could to be part of the group.

The class worked in small groups a lot, so Miss Langdon knew Pam would get a chance to have some one-on-one conversations.

Progress came slowly, but by the end of the quarter, the teacher could see a change in her students. Pam's classmates started laughing with her instead of at her, and they started working more as a group. Pam started handing out compliments rather than slams.

One day, Miss Langdon was walking down the hall before class and she heard a couple of students who weren't from the reading class making fun of Pam as she headed down the hallway. At the same moment, three of Pam's reading classmates happened by and heard the comments about Pam. "Leave her alone," one of the three told the other students. "She's cool. She's our friend."

▶ **The Problem:** Racial differences were dividing a class.

▶ **What the Teacher Did:** The teacher worked with students both individually and as a group to encourage respect for one another and more tolerant behaviors.

▶ **The Lesson:** By identifying a problem and working actively to solve it, the teacher made her classroom a safer place. In addition, she taught her students the importance of respecting one another and their collective role as a class. The teacher used elements of a Boys Town education method called Proactive Teaching to guide the class. We will discuss this teaching method and others later in this book.

◆ Armed with a Smile

Mary Ruth Granger had been teaching at the large high school for many years. Everyone said she was a no-nonsense lady who knew her job and did it well.

One day, as Mrs. Granger was starting class, she asked one of the students in the back of the room to stop talking.

"You old b---- ," the student shot back at her.

She glared at the youth for a moment. Then, in her trademark deadpan voice, said, "Don't you ever call me old!"

The class roared with laughter. The student stared at her, but said nothing. When Mrs. Granger asked the boy to stop by and see her after class, the laughter immediately stopped. Then she continued the day's lesson with no more interruptions.

▶ **The Problem:** The teacher faced a pretty typical classroom situation. A kid was talking in class, and she needed to get him to quiet down so she could begin teaching. She was facing a power struggle with the student.

▶ **What the Teacher Did:** Mrs. Granger made a good decision about when to use humor in the classroom. She wasn't a teacher who constantly cracked jokes, but when she did let a zinger go, her wry sense of humor shone through, yet she regained control in the classroom. And by requiring the student to see her after school, she gave him a consequence for acting inappropriately. She communicated to him that she wasn't going to rise to his bait, making it unlikely that he'll try something like that with her again.

▶ **The Lesson:** The teacher used humor to prompt her students to be quiet when class is beginning and also to signal to them that she would not tolerate name-calling in her classroom. Using prompts with students and setting tolerances will be discussed in detail in later chapters of this book.

◆ Drawing the Line

Steve Tatum had been teaching history in one of the city's largest high schools for nearly ten years. He was a tall man with a thin nose and a salt-and-pepper beard. He had piercing brown eyes and he was known for his straightforward teaching style and personality. He had only one classroom rule: Respect one another.

One afternoon, two boys came to class having an argument that had started at lunch time. In Mr. Tatum's classroom, another boy got involved in the argument, and before the teacher even had a chance to start class, the argument had escalated to two-against-one, with one youth yelling, "I'm gonna get you, man!"

Students had filed into the classroom and were standing around watching the fight. Mr. Tatum went to the classroom door and slammed it hard. The noise startled everyone, and the argument stopped for an instant.

The teacher seized the opportunity. "Everyone in your seats. NOW!" he boomed, making his voice as deep and loud as he could. "Sam, you sit up here today," he directed one of the boys who'd been in the argument to a seat near his desk.

"Tony, over there." He steered one of the other boys to a seat at a far corner of the room.

"Now, let's talk about what happened here today. You are young men, but you looked like little boys just now. Fussin' at each other and tryin' to be tough. Well all you've done is disappoint me and disappoint your classmates. We don't respect you right now and you obviously don't respect yourselves, otherwise you wouldn't behave like that.

"You know what? If you don't have respect, you got nothin'. It's like you don't exist. That's how important it is. You think about that."

The classroom was dead quiet. The teacher didn't say anything, just leaned on his desk at the front of the room and looked at each of the boys for what seemed like a very long time. Then Mr. Tatum turned to the rest of the class. "Do you understand what I'm saying about respect?"

The students nodded "Yes," or mumbled in agreement. Mr. Tatum went on with class then, ignoring the three students throughout the class period. The youths steered clear of each other after that.

▶ **The Problem:** An argument between several students threatened to bring class out of control.

▶ **What the Teacher Did:** The teacher used his no-nonsense manner and ability to command respect to stop the argument and bring the class back into his control. He also showed his students that a classroom should be a place where individuals are equal and respect one another.

▶ **The Lesson:** The teacher brought his students lessons about what his tolerance level is in the classroom and how that tolerance means

nothing less than equal respect for all members of the class. Tolerance levels are an important component of classroom management; they set the limits students need for structured learning. We will discuss tolerances later in this book.

◆ Changing the Classroom Environment

It was Valentine's Day when Henry Richardson told his principal that he needed to take a leave of absence for heart surgery. The principal assigned Mr. Richardson's biology classes to Marianne Johnson for the rest of the school year.

Mrs. Johnson had been working in the district as a substitute teacher since she'd taken a leave of absence herself last year for the birth of her second son.

Mrs. Johnson had some trepidation about taking over the classes. She loved teaching and had five years' experience in her own classroom, but Mr. Richardson's reputation as an educator was stunning. She worried that she wouldn't be able to engage the students.

Mrs. Johnson stopped by her new classroom on Thursday. Her teaching stint was to begin the following Monday. Mr. Richardson ran a tight ship. He had a pull-down map of the world attached to the front chalkboard, but no other posters or decorations in the classroom. His reference books were in a neat row on one counter, bound together by a set of cheap metal bookends.

She made some mental notes about what the classroom needed and returned to school on Saturday morning to transform the room into her classroom.

She dug her old ten-gallon aquarium out of the basement at home and bought some goldfish. She also bought some plants, including a huge ficus, and replaced the metal bookends with a set of pewter dolphin bookends she'd had for years.

Then, Mrs. Johnson put her "Continents Series" posters on the walls – huge brightly-colored photographs depicting each of the earth's seven continents. Around the room, she scattered her collection of Beanie Baby animals, organizing them by the continent they call home.

On Monday morning, the first-period biology class couldn't believe their eyes when they stepped into the classroom. "This is awesome," one girl said. "I can't believe this is the same place," another student said.

That Monday, Mrs. Johnson spent a little time at the beginning of each class introducing herself. She also announced a "Name the Fish" contest and posted a sign-up sheet for volunteers to feed the fish each day and water the plants each week. She was surprised when students clamored to put their names on the sheets.

As school ended about three months later, the principal commented on the turnaround in the grades and attitudes of Mrs. Johnson's students. While most students were getting decent grades with Mr. Richardson, the overall level of accomplishment increased with Mrs. Johnson. The changes in the classroom environment definitely made learning biology more inspiring for more students, the principal said.

▶ **The Problem:** Marianne Johnson felt she had a tough act to follow by taking over Mr. Richardson's classroom in the middle of the year, and in many ways she did face a big challenge. But the austere environment in his classroom and the authoritarian manner in which he taught gave Mrs. Johnson a great deal of room to make improvements that would benefit students.

▶ **What the Teacher Did:** Changing the classroom environment was an effective way for Mrs. Johnson to introduce herself and her teaching style to the classes she was taking over. The colorful posters, plants, fish, and even Beanie Babies engaged the students and made the study of biology more "real" for them.

▶ **The Lesson:** Making a change in a classroom environment can be a way to connect with students and increase the potential for learning. The changes don't have to be elaborate or expensive, and you can even involve students in the process, like having them help feed the fish.

◆ Time to Learn

Marvin was a youth who hadn't spent much time in school, so he wasn't thrilled to be in Teresa Jones' English class. Every day, he'd come to class and act out, eventually getting himself sent to the office.

One day, Mrs. Jones figured out what Marvin was doing. He really didn't want to be in class, and he actually preferred the office to the classroom, so he'd do things to get himself out of class.

Mrs. Jones went to her principal, Claire Montgomery, and laid out a plan she'd developed to see if she could break Marvin of acting out in class. She wanted to use "planned ignoring." She wanted to wait Marvin out, to put up with his behaviors in class in the hopes that he would abandon them when he found out that they weren't getting him out of the classroom.

"I know it's unorthodox," Mrs. Jones told Miss Montgomery, "but I think it just might work."

"Marvin's had an awful lot of office referrals," Miss Montgomery said. "Go ahead and give it a shot."

The next day, Mrs. Jones talked to her student. "Marvin, you won't be going to the office today."

He was stunned. "But I'll be so bad that you'll have to send me to the office," he said.

"No, Marvin," she said. "You need to stay in class and learn."

After class started that day, Marvin began to act out. First he put his head down on his desk, like he was sleeping. Mrs. Jones ignored it, and she prompted the class to ignore it, too, because, she said, "Marvin needs to be in class, just like the rest of us."

Then Marvin began making noises, but she and the class also ignored that. Mrs. Jones knew that Marvin was growing frustrated.

The next day, Marvin tried another tactic. He had Science class before English, so he acted out in Science class, earned an office referral, and managed to get the referral extended through English class.

When Mrs. Jones figured out what Marvin had done, she went to the Science teacher, Jim Hickman, and explained what she was trying to do. Mr. Hickman agreed not to send Marvin to the office. Even when Marvin stood on the lab table, Mr. Hickman ignored him and refused to send him to the office.

When Marvin got to English class that day – a Friday – he kept his head down almost the entire period. Mrs. Jones ignored him.

Once, when he looked up and began paging through his textbook, she said, "Marvin, good to have you with us. We're on page 144," and then immediately went back to teaching. She did not give him any extra homework or do anything else to punish him for acting out in class during this period.

On the following Monday, Marvin came to class and told Mrs. Jones, "I'm going to turn over a new leaf. I'm tired of messin' with you and Mr. Hickman."

"That's super, Marvin. I know it's been difficult for you, and I'm glad you'll be in class from now on," the teacher told the student. "Let's talk about how English class can be more interesting for you."

Marvin told the teacher he had problems reading Shakespeare, which the class was working on now, because of the differences in language. He said he often couldn't figure out what the story was about because he couldn't understand some of the language Shakespeare used.

Mrs. Jones said several other students had said the same thing and she'd given them a copy of "Tales from Shakespeare" by Charles and Mary Lamb. Mrs. Jones explained that the Lambs were a brother and sister writing team who had simplified Shakespeare's plays into stories that children could understand.

The teacher told Marvin that many adults read "The Lamb's Tales," as they are called, before digging into a Shakespeare play, so they can understand what's happening. She pulled out a copy of the book and gave it to Marvin.

"Take a look at this tonight and see if it helps. We'll talk about it in class tomorrow," the teacher said.

The book was a big help to Marvin. While he never became a big fan of Shakespeare, he was able to gain an acquaintance with the great writer, and he even remarked one day that "This Shakespeare guy sure knows a lot about people."

Marvin did better when the class started reading more modern classics. He came to class regularly and was good about sharing his experiences in class discussions. Mrs. Jones felt her greatest victory with Marvin was breaking his acting-out cycle and keeping him in class.

▶ **The Problem:** Mrs. Jones faced a difficult situation with Marvin. His refusal to participate in class became a test of wills between himself and his teacher.

▶ **What the Teacher Did:** In order to help Marvin be successful, Mrs. Jones had to put up with some inappropriate behavior to "wait out" Marvin so she could gain control and keep him in class. Having assistance from the Science teacher helped.

Keep in mind, however, that Mrs. Jones' strategy would not have worked with an extremely aggressive, volatile, or violent student who might have raised the ante in the classroom by doing something like threatening the teacher, throwing items around, or worse, creating an extremely dangerous situation. You must know your students well and have solid relationships with them before you embark on an experiment like this.

▶ **The Lesson:** Mrs. Jones had to find a creative strategy to handle Marvin's problem. Standard classroom expectations wouldn't work with this youth, who appeared to enjoy being on the periphery. She combined a variety of techniques to help the student, including prompting the other members of the class about what she was doing, trying to strengthen her relationship with Marvin, and using praise. The teacher also enlisted the help of another teacher in order to maintain the consistency of the intervention. This is an important component to help the student take behaviors learned in one setting and apply them to other situations. As students generalize behavior to different settings, they begin to see that rules remain the same, even if settings change. With consistent rules, students will not get mixed messages about what is tolerated and what isn't tolerated.

Note: The stories offered throughout this book are real. Some include strategies that depend on the teacher's relationship with the students. Others have strategies that could be counterproductive if overused. As always, teachers are urged to use good judgment, especially when working with aggressive or high-risk youth.

Understanding the Problem

Chapter Two

Dealing with Aggressive Youth

In the first chapter, we looked at some creative methods teachers employed to keep their classrooms safe from aggressive and violent students. In this chapter, we'll discuss the basics of aggression and how to identify it in your students. We'll also examine some distorted thinking patterns that can lead students to act out or behave aggressively, as well as some risk factors that make youngsters turn to aggression and violence. We'll also discuss protective factors, such as family stability, that reduce youths' susceptibility to relying on aggressive means to get their needs meet.

◆ Identifying Aggression

It's early October and teachers at Karen's school have grown increasingly frustrated with the freshman for her uncooperative attitude. She consistently refuses to follow instructions in the classroom and always has a sarcastic response when teachers ask her to participate in discussions or to answer a question.

Eric and Michelle went steady for two years, before Michelle broke off the relationship two months ago. She told Eric she wanted to date other guys. Since the breakup, Eric has been following Michelle after she leaves school, and he often sits in his truck outside the restaurant where she works and tries to talk to her when her shift ends. Michelle has asked Eric to leave her alone, but he says he loves her and just wants to be with her.

John gets in fights nearly every day at school. He's known for shoving kids into lockers if he feels they have somehow offended him. John never speaks softly. He always uses a loud, belligerent voice tone and frequently challenges his

classmates with "Whassup, Waterboy? What you lookin' at?" Because of this, most kids avoid him, not wanting to risk being the subject of his wrath.

The stories above show three different faces of aggression. Karen's noncompliance and sarcasm represents low-level aggression. Eric's stalking of Michelle, while not overtly aggressive, has great potential for violence. The example of John shows the blatant use of physical aggression.

Aggression comes in many forms. While it has varying levels of severity, it is rooted in a basic desire to hurt others in some way.

According to Lange and Jakubowski (1976), aggression is "directly standing up for one's personal rights and expressing thoughts, feelings, and beliefs in a way that is often dishonest, usually inappropriate, and always violates the rights of the other person."

Obviously, many behaviors fall within this definition: acts of defiance, fighting, taking something from someone, name-calling, pushing and shoving, hitting, kicking, and making fun of others. Some of these behaviors may be common in your school.

However, aggression becomes a serious problem when a pattern of such behaviors develops and a student routinely uses aggressive behaviors to get his or her needs met. The pattern can be identified when the behavior occurs with great frequency, is severe and intense, or lasts for extended periods of time before the youth regains self control. When this occurs, teachers must work with teens and their families to identify alternative, assertive behaviors to replace the aggressive behaviors so that they will not become a permanent personality trait.

◆ Causes of Aggression

But why are today's youngsters turning to such deadly and violent acts such as school shootings? Society is struggling to answer this tough question. It seems incomprehensible that kids could be killing and assaulting kids and adults, but it's occurring at an alarming rate. The causes are myriad – and complex. Some people cite the soaring divorce rate and single-parent homes; others say youth have become desensitized to violence by what they see in the movies, on television, and in video and computer games.

In addition, the glamorization of brutal conduct that dominates music lyrics and videos may be another factor. Others argue that the cause lies in the ready availability of weapons like guns and knives. Statistics show that one-third of all households have at least one gun. Use and abuse of alcohol and drugs also may lead to aggressive and violent behavior.

Separately, none of these factors is probably the root cause of aggression and violence. However, it is possible that a compilation of these factors strongly influences students who already have a propensity to use aggression and violence as a way of coping with life's obstacles. A student's aggressive and violent tendencies can be fueled and validated by all these influences. In other words, kids may be getting the message that it's okay to lash out in destructive and hurtful ways.

Biology (neurotransmitters and genetics) and psychosocial processes (thoughts and feelings) often have a direct impact on a youth's aggression and violence problem. However, Boys Town also believes that most students who choose aggression and violence have learned, often unwittingly, to use these kinds of abusive behaviors from parents and other influential adults.

These students have learned that aggression and violence are options for solving problems by seeing others who are important in their lives repeatedly use these behaviors. Many of these same aggressive and violent youngsters haven't had the opportunity to learn more positive ways of coping with and solving disagreements with others. Simply put, these kids just don't know any other way to handle difficult, frustrating, or upsetting situations that inevitably arise.

Aggression is a complex and difficult problem. There are no miracle "cures," and no one has an answer for every problem. Helping students overcome their aggression requires hard work, tenacity, and creativity.

The earlier you intervene against aggressive behaviors, the greater the chance your students will learn positive ways to interact with others and get what they want through socially acceptable channels. It is vital that teachers, parents, and other adults steer kids away from aggression and back to a path that can lead them to success at home, in school, on the job, and in life.

As a teacher, you've probably noticed that the severity of aggression in students varies. Some days, your most aggressive students may seem quite charming and sociable. This often happens when everything is "going their way." On other days, they seem to have no self-control at all. This is because many factors can affect how a youth behaves in different situations. The factors may range from major life events such as parents' divorcing, drug use, or a romance gone sour, to more minor occurrences such as someone teasing the youth in the hall or the fact that he or she stayed up too late the night before.

In the classroom, students typically use aggressive behaviors to get reinforcement from their peers or from adults. Youth also may turn to aggressive behavior if they grow frustrated with the curriculum being presented – if the lesson plan is too easy, leaving them bored, or if the lesson plan is too hard, giving them few opportunities for successful learning.

Often, when you determine how severe a student's aggression is, you have the starting point for identifying what kind of intervention will be needed to stop the behaviors. We will discuss intervention strategies later in this book.

◆ The Aggression Continuum

Aggression can develop along a continuum and vary in degrees. The behaviors along this continuum are diverse and drastically more harsh as youth move from lower-level behaviors like noncompliance and yelling to more overt actions like assault and murder.

Keep in mind, though, that as severity increases, the frequency of the behavior usually will decrease. For example, you might see a student frequently using low-level noncompliant behaviors like whining or being sarcastic, but a teenager using more overt types of aggression won't be so high profile because the behavior is more serious and the stakes are higher. A student involved in more serious aggressive behaviors like property damage or assault is going to behave more covertly than the mouthy teen who won't follow your classroom instructions. So keep your radar active. Don't get lulled into thinking that a youth has turned over a new leaf when what's really happening is that he's getting more aggressive. Later in this book, we'll discuss monitoring and supervision skills that will help you know how to keep an eye on students and prompt them to act appropriately.

No matter how aggressive a student is, however, the common factor that binds all these aggressive behaviors together is the end result: Kids get their way or get their needs met. Your job is to identify where a student is along the continuum and to help him or her find appropriate ways to have needs fulfilled.

But how do you determine the seriousness of a student's aggressive behaviors? Generally speaking, the least aggressive behaviors are those where a student is passive or is not following instructions and/or is making threatening statements or gestures.

Noncompliant behaviors might include a youth repeatedly refusing to do what a teacher asks, whining or crying, making sarcastic responses, and criticizing or teasing another.

Threatening statements might include actions such as issuing an ultimatum ("If you don't give me a pass, you'll be sorry."), staring and glaring, cursing and yelling, or making demanding statements ("Give me that book!"). Other behaviors in this category might include: repetitive verbal or nonverbal behavior that is intended to annoy (pounding a fist on a table), clenching fists, invading someone's personal space, physically aggressive posturing (towering over someone in a threatening manner), or uttering verbal threats.

From these types of behavior, youngsters may "up the ante" and begin engaging in more aggressive behaviors such as causing property damage, stealing, setting fires, or mistreating animals.

Then, their behaviors can escalate to those that can physically harm others or themselves, such as pushing or shoving, punching, fighting,

or trying to hurt themselves, such as carving their own skin. These behaviors may not produce long-lasting or permanent physical or psychological damage, but they are serious, are likely to elicit serious consequences, and need immediate attention.

As students grow more comfortable with aggressive behavior, they may experiment with serious animal cruelty. There is evidence to suggest that youth who repeatedly hurt animals or engage in ritualistic torture of animals move on to behavior that may seriously harm themselves or other people. For example, a youth charged in one of the U.S. school shootings was being investigated for allegedly torturing several cats, behavior that occurred prior to the shooting at the youth's school.

Therefore, a youth who regularly hits or kicks animals, or who engages in more serious behaviors such as poisoning, shooting, or setting an animal on fire, should definitely be considered at-risk for using extremely violent behaviors against humans.

Obviously the most dangerous aggressive behaviors youths engage in are behaviors that threaten humans with serious physical or psychological damage, such as stalking, bomb threats, terrorism, aggravated assault, rape, suicide, or murder.

As you can see, you need to be intensely aware of student behavior. An increase in intensity or severity of behavior often signals that your student is becoming more aggressive, and more dangerous – not only to others, but to himself.

Keep in mind that the behaviors we have listed here contain examples of just a few of the many types of behavior possible. Your students may be demonstrating other kinds of behavior. Having a good relationship with your students will give you insights into their personalities that may provide clues to how aggressive they are becoming.

And remember that kids may take different routes to becoming dangerous. Some youth who display the most overtly aggressive behaviors have done so in a sequential fashion, moving from a low-level behavior to one that is slightly more-dangerous. Other kids, however, might suddenly move from using a low-level behavior like whining and teasing to assault or rape or murder. With these students, there are few or no warning signs or clues that a youth is about to act in a highly aggressive or violent manner.

It is very important to remember that every student is different and each situation is unique. So – in the absence of any intervention – how slowly or quickly a youth's behaviors escalate is highly individualized and depends on many factors in his or her life.

Understanding and directly dealing with the day-to-day occurrences of less-severe aggressive behaviors such as not following directions and whining gives you, the teacher, a better chance of stopping those behaviors from escalating into hitting, vandalism, and in extreme cases, physical assault. Proactively teaching students self-control skills and other positive, alternative behaviors will give them tools to use when they find themselves lapsing into aggressive patterns.

Although crime statistics show that more youngsters are engaging in the most severe forms of aggressive behavior, including assaults and rapes, not all aggressive kids commit these extreme acts of violence. The majority of aggressive youth engage in more subtle types of aggression, such as glaring at a teacher while he or she is reviewing an assignment or standing menacingly close, invading personal space. School hallways are sometimes full of kids teasing, bullying, or "dissin'" other kids.

The Aggression Continuum

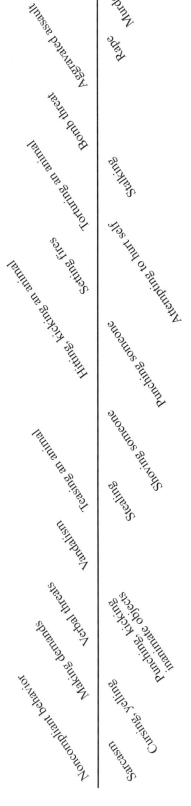

High Level Aggression

Murder
Rape
Aggravated assault
Bomb threat
Stalking
Attempting to hurt self
Torturing an animal
Punching someone
Setting fires
Shoving someone
Hitting, kicking an animal
Stealing
Teasing an animal
Vandalism
Verbal threats
Punching, kicking inanimate objects
Making demands
Cursing, yelling
Noncompliant behavior
Sarcasm

Low Level Aggression

Although outcomes often determine the seriousness of aggressive behaviors, school personnel must evaluate those behaviors on a case-by-case basis. The student's history, environment, and the presenting circumstances will determine the appropriate course of action to take.

> ### Aggression Facts
>
> - Youngsters who begin to use aggressive behavior early in life are much more likely to engage in severe forms of aggression and violence later in life.
>
> - Several factors that correlate with aggression in youth also hinder a youngster's ability to maintain self-control during stressful times. They include: verbal skills, problems in school, difficulty paying attention, and exposure to high levels of conflict at home and in the neighborhood.
>
> - Aggression and violence can be heavily influenced by family factors. Some of these factors include insecure attachment relationships between children and mothers, parental disciplinary practices that include physical punishment or unreasonably punitive discipline, single-parent homes, and violent neighborhoods.

Gangs lurk around corners, and aggressive language abounds.

Many times these low-level aggressive behaviors are overlooked or ignored because no one is getting physically hurt. Left unattended, however, these behaviors can be strengthened and actually escalate to more serious behaviors. They also contribute directly to a climate where dangerous things happen. Recognizing and working to eliminate these less aggressive behaviors can prevent kids from resorting to more severe forms of aggression, including violence.

Youth who learn and adopt these behaviors have trouble making and keeping friends, and they often have fragmented relationships with parents and siblings. Adults label them as "troublemakers" or as "dangerous." Eventually, well-intentioned people such as teachers, coaches, and youth group leaders grow frustrated and stop trying to help these young people. Instead, the adults turn their attention to others who want to learn.

Ultimately, students who choose aggression and violence fail in school, in the neighborhood, and at home. They even may become adults with no tools except aggression to make their way in the world. Spousal and child abuse, drug and alcohol abuse and dependency, robbery and assault become the norm, destroying all prospects of holding a good job, building a good marriage, or having a happy family.

◆ Types of Aggression: Proactive and Reactive

During the last three years, 14-year-old Bobby has been arrested for shoplifting clothes and shoes at mall stores, vandalizing the house of a girl who refused to be his girlfriend, trespassing on school property, and stealing an expensive mountain bike from the rack outside his school.

At school Bobby is considered a troublemaker. When he gets caught doing something he shouldn't be doing, he makes excuses and tries to sweet-talk his way out of detention and other negative consequences. When that doesn't work, he often gets angry and challenges his teachers. As a result, many of Bobby's teachers let him off the hook and dismiss punishments because they don't want to deal with his temper tantrums.

Bobby is big for his age and considerably taller and stronger than his classmates. Most students are afraid of him, and he uses his physical superiority to intimidate them. This allows him to get what he wants. Bobby often teases and threatens his classmates, and he always seems to be fighting. The only friends he has are older boys who also are labeled as "troublemakers" by teachers and parents.

At home, Bobby uses the same aggressive behaviors to get out of doing chores or other activities he doesn't like. His parents are fed up with him, and their attempts to punish him for negative behavior inevitably result in shouting matches. Bobby ends up winning these arguments because he yells and screams and threatens his parents. Eventually, they give up, and Bobby gets out of doing what he doesn't want to do.

Tina is a 16-year-old girl who recently was arrested for assaulting a teacher for the second time in 10 months. In the latest incident, Tina was arguing with her teacher over a detention for being late to class following lunch. It was the third time in three days that Tina had been late. Tina started making excuses and blamed another student for her tardiness. Then she refused to accept the detention and ignored her teacher's requests to calm down.

Eventually, Tina started to curse, shout, and verbally threaten her teacher. When the teacher asked Tina to leave the classroom and report to the office, Tina "lost it" and shoved the teacher over a chair, then started to hit and kick her. Tina even tried to choke the teacher, who suffered a gash on the back of her head and had to make a trip to the emergency room for stitches.

Other teachers describe Tina as a "bomb ready to explode." Most ignore her minor offenses so they won't have to deal with her explosive temper. Tina is an outcast at school and in her neighborhood. She overreacts to minor problems, and other kids don't want to spend time with her because she might lash out at any time. Tina has been involved in many fights in her neighborhood and at school. Usually, Tina doesn't start these fights, but she does escalate conflicts and doesn't try to avoid them.

Tina's parents are divorced, and she lives with her mother. At home, Tina regularly punches and kicks her younger brother, two sisters, and her mother.

In these examples, Bobby and Tina share many common problems. Both Bobby and Tina have learned that using aggressive behaviors is the most effective way to get what they want, escape trouble, or avoid something they don't want to do. But other kids don't like them, and they have few friends. Teachers are frustrated with or fearful of them, and their relationships with their parents and siblings are in shambles.

Despite their similarities, Bobby and Tina use aggression in different ways. In order to get his needs met, Bobby deliberately bullies and hassles others. In other words, he *initiates* situations where he uses aggressive behaviors.

Tina, on the other hand, *reacts* with aggressive behaviors to the actions of others. She tends to lose control of her emotions and actions without thinking of the consequences, and she rapidly explodes in angry outbursts when something gets in her way.

Dodge (1991) refers to these distinct types of aggressive behavior as **"proactive aggression"** (Bobby) and **"reactive aggression"** (Tina). Understanding the type of aggressive behavior a student is more likely to use is an integral part of teaching aggressive youth appropriate responses to situations that frustrate, anger, or upset them.

According to Dodge (1991), "Proactive aggression occurs usually in the form of object acquisition, bullying, or dominance of a peer." Kids who use proactive aggression tend to initiate aggressive acts. They are often labeled as "manipulators" or "bullies." Aggression in these youngsters is calculated. It serves the purpose of helping them reach a goal.

Youth who use proactive aggression tend to begin with lower level aggression, then "up the ante" when those behaviors no longer are successful. Because of this, you may see more than one kind of aggression from a youth in one interaction. If cursing doesn't work, for example, the youth may throw a punch at you.

Generally speaking, youths tend to use more proactively aggressive behaviors as they grow older. But you also will see their behavior escalate in response to conditioning. A student who is constantly verbally demeaned by his teacher may feel he has to do more than curse the next time there's a confrontation, in order to control the situation.

Proactive aggressive youth use whatever behavior they have learned works best with a particular individual, whether it is a low-level behavior like whining or more aggressive behavior like threatening others. Once they know what type of aggressive behavior works best with a person, they will begin with that kind of behavior at every subsequent interaction that involves conflict.

For example, they may verbally threaten a parent, but use a lower-level behavior like whining with a teacher. The key to identifying proactive aggression is determining whether intent is involved and whether the youth is deliberately using aggression as a tool to meet a goal.

Bullying is a common example of proactive aggression. Bullies have a positive attitude toward aggression and violence. They enjoy the physical and emotional pain they inflict in their quest to get what they want. Controlling others is a strong need that drives their behavior. They have little, if any, empathy for their victims. Contrary to popular belief, bullies do not suffer from low self-esteem. In fact, the opposite is true: Bullies have little anxiety and are very secure in their identity. They also tend to be impulsive (Olweus, 1996).

Dodge (1991) defines reactive aggression as displaying "anger or temper tantrums, with an appearance of being out of control." Youngsters with this type of aggression are upset by the actions and reactions of others and respond in an emotionally charged manner. Often, these youth are described as "having a short fuse" because they can quickly go from being calm to exploding in anger over a minor issue such as being told "No."

Youngsters who use aggression reactively are unable to control their actions when they become angry, frustrated or fearful. They are like the 2-year-old child who becomes angry and throws a tantrum because he can't have something he wants. That may be common for a 2-year-old, but it is not socially acceptable for an older youth.

Reactive aggressive kids tend to explode with extremely aggressive and, at times, violent behavior. They don't typically escalate their aggression in a sequential fashion, but usually move quickly to more severe types of aggression like cursing, verbal threats, punching, or fighting.

Like youngsters who are proactively aggressive, these youth can be outgoing and gregarious or quiet and passive, but their aggressive response to feelings of anger, frustration, or fear is unpredictable – sometimes even to themselves – and laden with emotion.

◆ Is Aggression Ever Justified?

So far, we have defined aggression in strictly negative terms. Aggression in students is a behavior that teachers want to prevent or reduce as they teach kids prosocial and positive ways to solve problems or get what they want. There are times, however, when aggressive behavior is both appropriate and necessary. This "justified aggression" – a type of reactive aggression – can include the use of verbal or physical force, and people most often resort to it in extreme situations where they must act to protect or defend themselves or others.

Consider this example: A girl is walking home from school when a stranger in a car pulls up to the curb and asks her for directions. When the girl approaches the car, the man suddenly grabs her arm. She reacts by screaming, scratching his face, and eventually biting his hand. The stranger lets go and drives off as the girl runs to the safety of a nearby house.

In this example, the girl probably was thinking that the man was going to kidnap and possibly kill her. This thinking led to feelings of fear, which resulted in the aggressive behaviors of screaming, scratching, and biting. But because she was acting out of self-preservation and self-defense, her actions were justified and appropriate.

Would these same behaviors be justified if the girl attacked her counselor because she wouldn't let the student drop algebra? Absolutely not. In this situation, the girl's thinking might be that her counselor is always mean and never fair. This could lead to feelings of anger and frustration, which result in the aggressive behaviors of screaming, scratching, and biting. In this case, the girl's thoughts, feelings, and behaviors would not be justified, and she likely would earn severe negative consequences.

Many students, particularly those from at-risk environments, use violent and aggressive behaviors as an all-purpose solution to get what they want. These behaviors have served them well in settings where they truly were in physical danger. Because they found success in these high-stakes situations, the students figure the behaviors will work equally well in other situations. In other words, these students "hyper-aggress" whenever they're confronted by a perceived threat.

Our job as teachers is to teach students how to use prevention methods to keep themselves safe and how to make assessments of the environment they're in to determine how safe it is. In addition, we must teach students that other options are available to solve problems and get what they want. See the "Code-Switching" section in the Proactive Teaching chapter for more information on this concept.

While students should be taught that they have the right to protect themselves or others, we want to stress that most aggression is undesirable and harmful. Obviously, students can choose to misuse this right, saying that they slugged another student because they felt threatened or in danger. In these situations, teachers, as well as parents, have to make a judgment call about whether the student's behavior is justified or not and respond accordingly.

◆ What Aggression Is Not

The continuum of severity in aggression and types of aggression provides a strong foundation for understanding what aggressive behavior is and the wide range of behaviors that comprise it.

However, it is important for teachers and others to recognize that there are certain areas where a youth's behavior might appear to be aggressive, but in reality it is not. Anger and assertiveness fall into this category.

Knowing what aggression is not enables teachers and other school staff to distinguish between appropriate behavior that should be praised and reinforced and harmful, aggressive behavior that requires intervention. Knowledge of these differences will have a tremendous impact on how you deal with a youngster's behavior and the treatment strategies you develop for the students in your classroom.

Anger and Aggression

Members of the swim team are looking forward to hosting a meet at their home pool Thursday. It will be the first time a meet has been held in the new pool. At a team meeting Tuesday, some team members say they have heard a rumor that some kids are going to dump red dye in the pool as a joke.

Some team members say they know the group of students behind the dye threat, and they're going to put the word out that dumping dye in the pool would mean cancellation of the meet – and that wouldn't be fair because the swim team has worked really hard to organize the meet.

On Thursday morning, the swim coach arrives at school early to find the swimming pool

water a deep cherry red. She immediately summons the principal, and they start calling other schools to cancel the swim meet.

The swim team members are angry. Some want to search out the suspects after school, but the team captain convinces them that that will only get them in trouble. After a long meeting, they decide to give the principal the names of people whom they believe were involved in the prank and let him investigate the situation.

Fifteen-year-old Tonya's twin brother, Tony, just got arrested for shooting another youth in the neighborhood. Tonya is feeling scared for her brother, but she's determined not to show anyone how she feels and to defend what Tony did to everyone. When she arrives at school the next day, she waits for someone to say something. She is ready to show everyone what happens if they "mess" with her. Few kids say anything to her because everyone knows Tonya might lash out at them, as she has many times in the past.

At lunch, Tommy, a new student, sits across from Tonya at the table. On a dare from some boys he wants to impress, Tommy catches Tonya's eye while she's eating and points a finger at her as if it were a gun. Then, with a snarl, he says, "Bang!"

"Stop dissin' me man," Tonya shouts, then picks up her lunch tray and throws it at Tommy, hitting him on the head. She climbs over the table and grabs Tommy's hair, trying to pull it out in clumps. Within seconds, both youths fall to the floor, where Tonya starts to punch, kick, and bite Tommy.

It takes three teachers to pull Tonya off Tommy. He ends up with a cut on his cheek, a swollen eye, and a bite mark on his arm that requires stitches. Tonya is expelled from school;

the fight is the last straw in a long list of incidents where she verbally or physically attacked classmates and teachers.

In the two examples, members of the swim team and Tonya are justified in feeling angry. Most youngsters would be mad if an important meet had to be canceled or if someone teased or made fun of them. However, what sets these students apart is how they reacted when they felt angry.

The difference between anger and aggression is that anger is a feeling, while aggression is a behavior or set of behaviors. The same distinction exists with other emotions. For example, sadness is a feeling, but crying is a behavior, a way to express sadness. However, just as one can be sad without crying, a person also can be angry without being aggressive. The important point here is that there is nothing wrong with feeling angry, unless you express the anger in aggressive or violent ways that violate the rights of others.

The swimmers' actions following their initial feelings of anger were appropriate, socially acceptable, and healthy ways to handle what happened. The end result was that there was no serious aggressive behavior, no one was hurt, and the proper authority – the principal – dealt with the problem of the dye in the swimming pool.

Even though the swimmers were angry, they still were able to make a good decision to let the principal handle the problem, rather than create consequences for themselves by going after the alleged offenders themselves.

Tonya's feelings of anger resulted in dangerous, antisocial, and violent behaviors. Her way of reacting to situations when she gets mad is to strike out in destructive and harmful ways. This results in many negative consequences, including her expulsion from school. Other consequences might include alienation from friends and teachers and relationship problems at home. Obviously, Tonya's use of high-level aggressive and violent behaviors warrants immediate professional intervention.

Remember: Anger is a feeling, aggression is a behavior. It's normal for youngsters to get mad. However, many youngsters have learned to respond to feelings of anger with aggressive and violent behaviors. These are the kids who need help in learning new, appropriate ways to focus their anger.

Assertiveness and Aggression

Janice is a 15-year-old student who earns excellent grades in all her classes. Her goal is to receive all A's during high school so she can earn a college scholarship. But Janice's teachers and classmates don't like her very much because she's so obnoxious.

Janice constantly bombards her teachers with irrelevant questions. She also verbally challenges them on everything from simple class rules to the grades she receives on tests. This always happens during class time and takes a lot of teaching time and attention away from other students. Janice's teachers have asked her to come to them after class with her questions, but she ignores their requests and demands answers immediately.

Janice's classmates are frustrated because she dominates the teachers' time. When tests and other assignments are returned, Janice pesters other students about what grades they received and she constantly boasts about her high marks.

Mark is new at Somerset High School this year.

After taking his first math test, Mark discovered that his teacher marked four problems wrong that actually were right. He re-checked his work just to be sure, then approached the teacher, Mr. Johnson, after class and asked if he could discuss the test with him. Mr. Johnson agreed.

Mark showed him the four problems he thought were correct, and Mr. Johnson agreed that he had marked the problems wrong by mistake. "I must have been distracted when I was grading your test," he told Mark. Then the teacher apologized for his mistake and thanked Mark for bringing the problem to his attention. After that, Mark and Mr. Johnson often joked about the situation. It helped them establish a good relationship that lasted throughout the year.

Assertiveness is defined by Lange and Jakubowski (1976) as "…standing up for personal rights and expressing thoughts, feelings, and beliefs in *direct, honest, and appropriate* ways which do not violate another person's rights." This is exactly the opposite of aggression.

An integral part of assertiveness is respect. More specifically, this involves respect for one's own needs and rights, as well as for the needs and rights of others. Assertiveness is not simply a way to get what you want. It's a two-way street where the needs and rights of everyone involved are taken into consideration.

In the examples of Janice and Mark, Janice appears to be acting assertively because she is expressing her thoughts in direct and honest ways. But her behaviors are not appropriate, because she is ignoring her teachers' requests not to waste class time, which hurts her classmates.

High Risk Student Factors

Jeffrey Sprague, Ph.D., of the University of Oregon College of Education's Institute on Violence and Destructive Behavior, identified the following student factors related to a high risk for violence and delinquency. A youth need not have all of these risk factors, but the more a youth has, the higher the risk he or she will face.

- Poor social skills
- Poor school engagement
- Family with one or more of the following characteristics: lack of parental supervision, mother or father ever arrested, evidence of child abuse or neglect, at least one family transition such as divorce or remarriage, death, or other trauma affecting family members
- Pre-delinquent problem behaviors such as bullying and annoying others, fighting, being stubborn and defiant, and telling lies
- Early drug and alcohol use
- Early onset age of delinquent activity
- A high level of "Daily Hassles" (minor stressors)
- Attention Deficit Hyperactivity Disorder
- Learning disabilities
- Low IQ, especially verbal ability
- Poor school performance, especially poor grades in high school
- Delinquent peers
- Having multiple risk factors: The cumulative effect of several family and child risk variables has been found to be a better predictor of delinquency than any single variable alone

In fact, much of Janice's behavior could be considered low-level forms of aggression, including making demanding statements. These behaviors require correction from teachers and the other adults in Janice's life.

On the other hand, Mark demonstrated assertive behavior in resolving his issues with Mr. Johnson. Mark stood up for his own rights in an appropriate way and respected Mr. Johnson's rights by calmly discussing the matter with the teacher after class. Mark's respectful assertive approach contributed to a favorable outcome.

If you're uncertain whether a youngster's behavior is assertive or aggressive, ask yourself if the youth is standing up for his or her rights in honest and appropriate ways that also respect the rights of others. If the answer is "No," then intervention is needed to help the youth learn a more responsible way to get what he or she wants.

◆ Risk and Protective Factors

What makes a student aggressive or violent? A variety of personal, family, and societal factors frequently converge to produce violent behavior patterns in youth. An acquaintance with these factors may help you identify some of your students who are likely to adopt antisocial behaviors and to act out aggressively or use violent means to solve problems.

Risk factors are all around us – from our family makeup to societal influences (Walker, 1998).

Family-based risk factors include the following: little supervision of youths' activities, whereabouts, or friends; lack of discipline and use of harsh discipline; family pressures that impact kids, such as unemployment, alcohol and drug use, and domestic violence (Patterson, Reid, & Dishion, 1992).

School-based risk factors might include outdated classroom materials that fail to engage students' interest, tolerance levels that are too high, or a detached staff.

Neighborhood and community-based risk factors identified by the Office of Juvenile Justice and Delinquency Prevention include: high crime rate, unsafe neighborhoods, lack of social cohesion among residents, few after-school or recreation activities for youth, and lack of connection between the school and the community it serves.

And society at large also has an impact on how many violent behaviors youth make their own through influences such as violence portrayed in the media, growing incivility, social fragmentation, and concepts of right and wrong that are increasingly portrayed as relative rather than clear-cut (Hughes & Hasbrouck, 1996).

Together, these risk factors are contributing to a generation of youth who see violence as a viable method to solve problems, don't respect the rights of others, aren't socially responsible, don't have basic social skills and manners, and don't value human life (Walker, 1998).

Youth inevitably will bring those attitudes and behaviors with them to school, creating problems for classmates and school staff. Later chapters of this book will contain useful techniques for grappling with those behaviors and teaching youth appropriate alternative behaviors.

Early intervention is crucial to diminish the effects of these risk factors because research has shown that the presence of the factors signals trouble later for the student. For example, Walker, Colvin, and Ramsey (1995) conducted a study that followed a group of boys. The study found that certain risk factors, if present in fifth grade, could fairly accurately signal trouble for the students five years later.

The risk factors – weak social skills, a higher than normal frequency of in-school discipline referrals from teachers, and a high rate of negative, aggressive behavior directed toward peers on the playground – were highly predictive of arrests in 10th grade.

By identifying students with risk factors, you can help route them toward success in school and hopefully keep them from dropping out or getting in trouble with the law.

But the news is not all bad when it comes to at-risk students. Sprague (1999) identified several protective factors – some school-based – that act as buffers against the risk of developing violent and destructive behavior patterns. They are listed below.

- Family stability
- Positive temperament
- Academic success
- Positive school experiences
- Positive work or work training experiences
- High self-esteem
- Structure in the environment (school and home)
- A good relationship with a parent or other adult
- Advanced self-help and problem-solving skills
- Internal locus of control (anger management, limit setting, goal setting)
- An identified network of family and friends who are available for support in a crisis

- High engagement in positive activities (e.g. sports, hobbies, art, community service)

This book contains information about several protective factors listed above. See Chapter 7 on Forging Relationships with Students for a discussion of how you can forge trusting relationships with students. See Chapters 10 and 11 for information on problem-solving and self-control strategies for students.

◆ Distorted Thinking Patterns

Often the flames of a youth's aggression are fanned by distorted thinking. Known as cognitive distortions, these skewed thinking patterns trip up young people with thoughts such as "I know he's out to get me" or "I'm always the one who gets blamed." Operating from these false impressions, the teenager frequently loses his temper or takes some action resulting in negative consequences.

Kids use cognitive distortions to get their way. Youth who are proactively aggressive tend to use the distortions to gain some kind of positive outcome for themselves, whereas youth who are reactively aggressive usually use the distorted thinking to escape something they don't want to do.

Cognitive distortions undermine the student's ability to perceive what others are experiencing and to read the cues that others are providing. There are four common cognitive distortions that aggressive students use (McKay, Davis, & Fanning, 1981). They are:

▶ **Arbitrary Inference:** Misperceiving a social cue or "mind-reading" another's intentions; in other words, drawing a conclusion from insufficient or contradictory information.

An example would be a situation where Bob is struggling to climb a rope ladder in gym class. When another youth offers to lend him a hand up the ladder, Bob angrily says "Shove it!" Although the offer is genuine, Bob perceives that the other student is asking to help only so that he can make fun of Bob in front of the other kids.

▶ **Magnification:** Exaggerating the meaning of an event or catastrophizing (making a mountain out of a molehill). For example, Patty is caught cheating on a test. Although she's disappointed at getting caught, she does not feel it's fair that she receives a detention. She begins to rant and rave, yelling, "I've never had a detention. You're ruining my whole life. I won't even be able to go out this weekend." She then begins to swear and tells the teacher that she better "back off."

▶ **Dichotomous Reasoning:** Overly simplified and rigid perceptions of events as all or nothing, or always or never. For example, Jermaine wants to go to a concert with some friends, but his parents won't give him permission because they don't approve of the musical group. Jermaine gets angry and yells, "You never let me do anything!" He rushes out the front door and slams it shut behind him.

▶ **Overgeneralization:** Taking a single incident, such as failure, as a sign of total incompetence. Consider this example: Karen, a new student at Upper Valley High School, doesn't get one of the lead roles in the fall musical. She tells her mother she wants to quit the drama club because she knew she wasn't going to be any good.

Students who engage in distorted thinking will need many helpful conversations with teachers and other concerned adults. They will need much encouragement to change not only their behavior but also how they see the world. Remember, their world view is part of the problem.

When a student stomps off the basketball court or blows up in the classroom, you will need to talk with him, not just to calm him down, but to help him see a different side of the situation. Start asking questions to gently draw him out.

"Talk to me a little about what happened today, Evan."

"I missed that shot, so we lost the game."

"Why do you think you missed the shot?"

" 'Cause I can't shoot free throws. I'm just no good. I'm gonna quit the team."

"If you could improve your free throw average, would you still quit?"

"No, but I can't. I'll never be any good at it."

"Well, what have you done to try? Have you practiced every night after school? Have you thrown 50 free throws every night for a week? Have you figured out how many of those you could make if you just kept practicing ?"

"No."

"Well I don't think you've shot enough free throws to give up yet. Right now I'm thinking this was a bad day. I'm thinking maybe you should practice some more and then decide. What do you think?"

"I guess you're right."

A conversation such as the one above might be a way to redirect a student's thinking from his perceived problem – lack of ability, to the actual problem – lack of practice. You can use similar sets of questions to help your students get back on track when distorted thinking carries them away.

If a student has hurt someone else because of behavior stemming from distorted thinking – shoving or yelling at someone, for example, – having the student apologize is another crucial part of the process to clear up thinking patterns. An apology is the student's verbal acknowledgment that his or her view of the circumstances was wrong.

See Chapter 4 on Thinking, Feeling, and Behaving for more information on how distortions in thinking can cause problems for students. Here is a list of other steps that you can use to talk with students about how they can restructure the distortions in their thinking:

▶ **Recognize physical responses to anger.** At a neutral time, try to help the student identify what physical symptom appears when he or she first begins to feel anger. The symptoms might include sweaty palms, clenched teeth, stiffening of the shoulders, flushed face, etc. The student may have a difficult time defining a particular symptom, and you may need to watch closely the next few times he or she gets angry to see if you can help identify it. Once the youth is aware of this first physical symptom of anger, he or she can go on to the following steps.

▶ **Stop and make a self-calming statement.** Help the student to understand that as soon as he experiences that first physical symptom of anger, he should tell himself to stop, and then he should say something to himself that is calming, such as "It's going to be okay; just take a second to calm down" or "This may not be as bad as I think. Let me calm down for a second." Another self-calming statement suggestion is "Okay, just count to 10 and stay calm." We will discuss other self-control strategies later in this book.

▶ **Evaluate the thoughts.** Help the student see that she sometimes has a thought that is not accurate before she becomes aggressive. Try to talk the student through recent aggressive situations to help her identify what that initial thought may have been. Once the student understands how this happens, she can learn how to make the self-calming statement, and then try to figure out what thought occurred before she began to feel anger. Teach the student to identify the distortion. Examples of such thoughts include "She just hates me" or "It's his fault that I missed the ball." Also, many of us have basic, common "put-downs" for ourselves that are distorted. So, the youth could be thinking something such as "I never do anything right" or "I'm just stupid."

Once the distortion is identified, teach the student to make a self-statement to address the distortion. Examples of such statements include:
- "Maybe she doesn't really hate me. She might be trying to help me."
- "It might not be his fault I missed the ball. He may have overthrown it by accident."
- "I'm not dumb. I just make mistakes like everyone else."

▶ **Think about options, and choose one.** Teach the student to take a few minutes to think about his options before reacting. Remind the student about the consequences of choosing to become aggressive, and tell him to think about all the alternative ways he could react in this situation. Teach the student to choose a positive alternative from the options and try it. Emphasize that he will not know if alternatives will work unless he is willing to give them a try. Explain that other alternatives often can have pleasant results, and that if the teenager is willing to take a risk, he will experience some of these over time.

▶ **Develop a self-corrective process.**
Help the student learn how to document situations that occur and how to share them with you. Ask questions and help the student explore whether or not she was able to change the distorted thinking and if she feels comfortable with the outcome. It is extremely important that you praise and reinforce the student for any effort to change her thinking, even if she doesn't select the best choice possible. Remember, all change takes time. Do not expect success immediately or consistently.

▶ **Look at the other person's perspective.** While the student is thinking about past situations, have him document the perspective of other people who were involved. Tell him to write down what he thought the other person was thinking and feeling. Getting aggressive youth to see other people's perspectives is important. If they distort the other person's point of view, help them to see how things really were. If a student can develop empathy for others, he is far less likely to engage in abusive behavior.

▶ **Don't expect perfection:** Remind the student that change is difficult for everyone. Tell her that she should try to remember a couple of these steps at first. Eventually, she will be able to do all the steps. Encourage the student not to lose heart if she doesn't do it exactly right the first time.

▶ **Set goals.** The aggressive student needs realistic goals. If a student has been "blowing up" in the classroom twice a week, trying to reduce that to one "blowup" a week might be a

reasonable goal to start with. Chart the frequency of the behavior, and discuss progress with the student daily. Be sure to give lots of encouragement and praise.

A final word about offering encouragement to students: your best success will come with youngsters with whom you have developed a relationship. One of the most positive aspects of relationship-building is that it can be used to reinforce a youth for controlling his or her own behavior. If a student feels close to you and likes you, he or she is more likely to want to please you. See Chapter 7, Forging Relationships with Students, for information about developing and nurturing relationships with students.

Chapter Summary

Identifying Aggression

Definition: Standing up for your rights in a way that is often dishonest, usually inappropriate, and always violates the rights of others.

Aggression becomes a problem when a student regularly uses aggressive behaviors to get his/her needs met.

Many factors, including social and biological influences, have an impact on use of aggressive behaviors.

Aggressive behaviors range from mild, characterized by noncompliant behaviors or making threatening statements to severe, which involves physically harming others or self.

Causes of Aggression

The Aggression Continuum

Types of Aggression

Proactive: A student initiates situations where he/she uses aggressive behaviors.

Reactive: A student reacts with aggressive behaviors to the actions of others.

Is Aggression Ever Justified?

What Aggression Is NOT

Anger: Anger is a feeling; aggression is a behavior or set of behaviors.

Assertiveness: Assertiveness is standing up for personal rights and expressing thoughts, feelings, and beliefs in direct, honest and appropriate ways that do not violate another person's rights. Assertiveness is the exact opposite of aggression.

Risk Factors that Lead to Aggressive Behavior

Includes poor social skills, drug or alcohol use, broken family

Protective Factors that Shield Students from Aggressive Behavior

Includes family stability, academic success, high self-esteem

Distorted Thinking Patterns

Cognitive Distortions: Including arbitrary inference, magnification, dichotomous reasoning, over-generalization

Restructure the distortions by recognizing physical responses to anger, making self-calming statements, evaluating thoughts, and developing a self-corrective process.

Chapter Three

The Conflict Cycle

It's Wednesday morning at 8:30, and Jessie, a sophomore, is just arriving at school. She's late, and she doesn't have a written excuse. Jessie is feeling frustrated because she knows she'll have to do an hour detention after school for her unexcused late arrival. That detention means she won't be able to play in today's softball game. It's an important game against Mount Hope High, a strong league rival.

When Jessie arrives in the school office, Assistant Principal Steve Taylor greets her. "Good morning, Jessie. What can we do for you this morning?"

"I need a pass, Mr. Taylor. I'm late 'cause I stayed up late working on my history report, and then I overslept and missed the bus. Is there any way I can do a detention tomorrow instead of today so I can play in the game this afternoon?"

"Sorry, Jessie. You know what the rules are. Detentions are to be served on the day they're earned. I'll write you up a pass. What class have you got first hour?"

Jessie angrily throws her backpack on the floor. It lands with a loud thud, startling several secretaries and students in the office. In a loud, angry voice, she says, "You can check my f------ card if you want to know what class I've got! This place ain't nothin' but a prison! It's not fair!"

Mr. Taylor says firmly, but kindly, "Jessie, I know you're upset, but using inappropriate language doesn't make things better for you. Now your card says you have English class first hour with Mr. McKinney. Here's your pass. And here's your detention slip for this afternoon."

In her anger, Jessie has started to sob, and she's embarrassed to have the office staff see her cry. She wipes her eyes with the sleeve of her jacket and says angrily, "You're a bunch of a-------! I'm getting out of here!" She grabs her backpack and moves toward the door as Mr. Taylor says, "Not so fast, young lady. Report to my office RIGHT NOW!"

Jessie turns defiantly to the assistant principal and glares at him as she pulls her back-

pack from her shoulder. Then she swings it in front of her as if it were a bat, and "Smack!" it hits the glass trophy case near the office door. Broken glass flies through the air and trophies tumble from the case. Jessie is suspended from school on the spot.

The story above illustrates researcher Nicholas Long's "Conflict Cycle." Long, as well as researcher Gerald Patterson, has developed theories that seek to explain how youth have learned to deal inappropriately with conflict and how teachers and other adults can effectively work with these youth.

◆ The Conflict Cycle: A Description

To understand why kids respond to some social situations with anger, aggression, and a loss of self-control, let's look at the "Conflict Cycle." Long believes that when a youth's behavior turns aggressive, the root cause usually lies in some unresolved incident. The incident arouses strong emotions in the youth and others who were involved, and even a minor incident can spiral into a major crisis.

According to Long, crisis is the product of a youth's stress that is kept alive by the actions and reactions of others. When a youth's feelings are aroused by stress, the youth learns to behave in ways that shield him or her from painful feelings. These behaviors are inappropriate, but they protect the youth from undesirable, distressing feelings. Others (parents, teachers, peers) perceive the youth's behavior as negative, and they respond in a negative fashion toward the youth. This negative response from others produces additional stress, and the youth again reacts in an inappropriate manner to protect himself or herself from further hurtful feelings. If unbroken,

this spiraling action-reaction cycle causes a minor incident to escalate into a crisis. This entire process is called the Conflict Cycle.

The Conflict Cycle follows this pattern: The first step is a stressful event (e.g., frustration, failure, rejection, and so on) that triggers a troubled student's irrational or negative beliefs (e.g. "Nothing good ever happens to me!"; "Everybody's out to get me!"). Negative thoughts determine and trigger negative feelings and anxieties, which drive the youth's inappropriate behavior. The inappropriate behaviors (e.g. yelling, screaming, threatening, sarcasm, etc.) incite others, who not only pick up the youth's negative feelings but also frequently mirror the youth's negative behaviors. This adverse reaction by others increases the youth's stress, triggers more intense feelings, and drives more negative behavior. The youth's behavior leads to even more anger and frustration on the part of the people around him or her. This cycle continues until it escalates into a no-win power struggle. Long says of the cycle: "Logic, caring, and compassion are lost, and the only goal is to win the power struggle."

In the end, the youth's irrational beliefs (e.g., "Nothing good ever happens to me; "Everybody is out to get me!") that started the Conflict Cycle sequence are reinforced, and the youth has no reason to change his or her irrational beliefs and inappropriate behaviors.

◆ The Conflict Cycle in Action

Let's look at the story above to see how the Conflict Cycle works:

Jessie is late for school and does not have a written excuse *(event creating stress, cycle 1 begins).*

Conflict Cycle

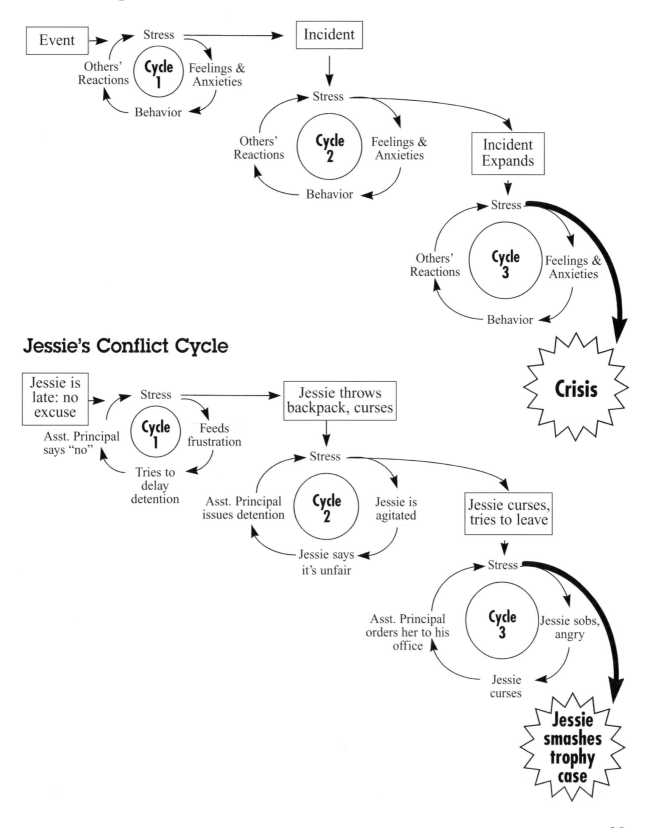

Jessie's Conflict Cycle

School policy states that students must stay after school for one hour if they do not have a legitimate written excuse. The youth is frustrated because if she has to stay after school, she'll miss the softball game *(feelings/anxieties)*.

Jessie makes an excuse, attempting to delay her detention to the next day *(negative behavior)*.

Mr. Taylor, the assistant principal, tells Jessie that the rule is non-negotiable, that detentions must be served on the day they are earned *(others' reactions creating more stress, cycle 2 begins)*.

Becoming agitated *(feelings/anxieties)*, Jessie throws down her backpack and curses at the assistant principal, saying that she's being treated unfairly *(negative behavior)*.

The teacher responds by telling her that using inappropriate language won't help her *(others' reactions creating more stress, cycle 3 begins)*.

Fighting back sobs *(feelings/anxieties)*, Jessie curses again at the office staff and tries to storm out *(negative behavior)*.

The assistant principal orders Jessie to his office, which will result in a call home *(others' reactions creating more stress, crisis)*.

Now, Jessie is extremely frustrated over the additional consequence. She picks up her backpack and swings it into the trophy case by the office door, sending flying glass across the room. She ends up with a suspension.

◆ Thoughts, Feelings, and Behaviors: The Building Blocks of the Conflict Cycle

The Conflict Cycle illustrates the interconnectedness of thoughts, feelings, and behaviors, an important concept students need to grasp as they begin to learn life's great lessons of dealing with consequences, maintaining self-control, and learning to solve problems.

At the core of this discussion are the three foundational pegs of the Conflict Cycle – thoughts, feelings, and behaviors.

The way we perceive a situation – the way we *think* and *feel* about it – more often than not governs how we will behave.

Take Jessie, for example. Her thoughts and feelings about the detention spawned frustration and anger, which fueled an escalating series of inappropriate behaviors that brought her a suspension.

Unfortunately, kids find themselves in these situations all the time because they do not yet have the broad range of personal life experiences and exposure to the ways of the world. Because of this lack of experience, their read on a situation may be completely off, and that will drive their behavior off course, too. Then, they find themselves facing negative outcomes or consequences.

Although all youth struggle with these issues, kids with aggressive and violent tendencies often have more difficulty because they have problems distinguishing behavior between different settings. No one has successfully taught them, for example, that you act differently in the classroom than you do on the streets of your neighborhood.

So how do you teach students to see their own Conflict Cycles – to see the connections between their thoughts, feelings, and behaviors – so they will be able to better predict the consequences of their actions?

There's a wonderful piece of streetwise advice that says "Check yourself before you wreck yourself." In a nutshell, that's what you're teaching. Your goal is to get your students to stop and examine their thoughts and feelings before they commit themselves to a behavior that will bring negative consequences.

Usually the best place to start with kids is to get them to look at behaviors they are using, since behaviors are more concrete than thoughts and feelings. Starting with behaviors, you can usually help students backtrack from there to identify the thoughts and feelings that seem to repeatedly spawn those behaviors.

For example, say you have a student who always overreacts when you give him an instruction in class. You might want to talk with him about working on those overreactions, and then, when one happens, walk him through it so he can see what thoughts and feelings drive his behavior. The following story illustrates this process.

◆ ◆ ◆

Teacher Phyllis Boyd has just asked Kevin Monroe, a sophomore, to turn around in his seat and stop chatting with the student behind him. Kevin jumps out of his seat and says, "What is up with you? You're ALWAYS on my case!" Then, he plops back in his seat and buries his face in his textbook.

Mrs. Boyd continues on with the class, saying, "Thanks for sitting down, Kevin. Now, let's take out our books and turn to page 256."

With about five minutes left in the class period, when her students are working independently, Mrs. Boyd asks Kevin if they can visit for a few minutes. When Kevin agrees, the teacher again praises him for promptly sitting down, especially since it was difficult for him. Then she begins to work with the student to get him to analyze why he let his temper erupt.

"Kevin, when I asked you to turn around in your seat, you said, 'You're always on my case.'

Let's visit about that a minute. What did you mean by that?"

The student pauses before he speaks. "I don't really know. I just feel like you're always doggin' me about my homework, and I don't get this s---."

"Kevin, if it seems like I'm on your case a lot, it's because I feel like you could be a better student. And I'm concerned about that. But what I'm more concerned about is that you're showing me your temper rather than showing me that you can be available for help. Let's talk about that.

"Earlier, you got bent out of shape when I asked you to do something. That's happened before. It looks to me like you have difficulty when someone gives you an instruction. That seems to trigger your temper. If you can learn to recognize when that happens, you can start to bring your temper under control."

"I just don't want people to push me around. My old man used to do that to me all the time."

"That's understandable, but maybe it would help if you start to think of instructions differently. Most of the time, when people ask you to follow an instruction, it is to accomplish something, like paying attention in class, or doing work around the house. Think of an instruction as something that needs to be done because you're part of a class or part of a family, not something that someone is demanding you do.

"Now, I'll admit that sometimes people give instructions when they're in a hurry or they're angry. In those cases, instructions seem like demands, and you feel like you're being ordered around. I can understand how you feel in those situations, but here's a tip – try to think about what they're asking, rather than how they're asking it. If people seem like they're bossing you around, you have the power to not react to their voice tone and just follow through and do the

job. You can still be responsible, and you don't have to get caught up in their bad day. Does that make sense?"

"Yeah, I see what you're saying."

"So when somebody tells you something, think about the instruction, not about the person giving the instruction. Then, before you do anything, take a deep breath, or count to three, or whatever you need to do to keep yourself from reacting negatively to the request. Then, follow through with the task and look at the situation afterward and see if you like how you handled it. Will you give that a try?"

"I guess."

"Good deal. I'll be ready to help if you want."

"Okay, thanks."

"Thanks, Kevin."

◆ ◆ ◆

◆ Analyzing the Conflict Cycle

In the story above, Mrs. Boyd helped Kevin see that his problem behavior (losing his temper) grew out of his strong negative feelings about being ordered around, which is how he believed his father dealt with him.

The teacher also helped Kevin to "reframe" the situation – to think about it in a different way. She tried to get Kevin to see that doing what someone asks is not being pushed around; doing what someone asks is just part of your role as a member of a family, a class, or other group.

This "reframing" is just one of the steps in teaching youth to maintain self-control. Reframing addresses the "thinking" part of the Thoughts-Feelings-Behavior triad. Reframing is where you ask your students to think about their

behavior in a new way so they can begin to replace negative behavior with more appropriate ways of acting.

To address the "feelings" part of the triad, you would talk to your student about maintaining emotional control. You might, for example, teach a student with a quick temper to start talking to himself when he begins to feel his anger rising. He might say something to himself, such as "I'm not going to feel bad or get angry just because things aren't going my way."

To address the "behaviors" part of the triad, you would work with a student to teach him or her how to replace inappropriate behaviors, such as throwing something, with a more appropriate behavioral response, like asking to be excused for some "cool down" time or simply taking a deep breath and following the instruction given.

As you can see, the process of teaching kids self-control is many-layered, but it is one of the more essential life skills they will ever learn. It is essential not only because it teaches youth appropriate ways to get their needs met, but also because it shows them that it's okay to ask for help when they need it. Too often, kids feel like they're the Lone Ranger, dealing with demands of friends, family, and school all on their own. Later in this book, we'll introduce some specific examples of self-control strategies that are used at Boys Town.

You can use the principles of Proactive Teaching, explained in Chapter 9, to structure your discussions with students about thoughts, feelings, and behaviors. The principles of Proactive Teaching work particularly well as you discuss with students the importance of switching behaviors as they move from one environment to another.

You also can use Proactive Teaching techniques in discussions about how language reflects behavior. For example, if you are working to reduce the use of "whiny" behavior in your classroom, you might talk with students about word choice and voice tone – about what they say and how they say it. Show them the difference between the plaintive wail "We never get to do fun stuff!" and the more positive question "Can we make some suggestions for new class activities?"

In some schools, counselors may work more closely with students than classroom teachers on these self-control issues. If that's the case in your school, you, as a classroom teacher, probably will take on a kind of "profiler" role for your counselors, providing them with information about the student that could provide some clues to what makes the student tick and what his or her "triggers" are.

In the following chapter, we will discuss the fundamental concepts behind thinking, feeling, and behaving, with some suggestions on how you can use them to help your students gain control over their personal Conflict Cycles.

Chapter Summary

The Conflict Cycle: A Description

Crisis is product of youth's stress that is kept alive by the actions and reactions of others.

The Conflict Cycle in Action

The Building Blocks of the Conflict Cycle

Thoughts
Feelings
Behavior

Analyzing the Conflict Cycle

ChapterFour

Thinking, Feeling, and Behaving

The last day of school is coming up soon, and Kyra thinks it would be nice to do something to make her favorite teacher's day special. Acting on those feelings of affection for her teacher, Kyra goes to the mall and buys her teacher a beautiful pottery mug and a greeting card. On the card, she writes "Thank you for being my teacher."

A teenage girl is walking down the hallway at school. As she passes two other girls, she sees one whisper something to the other. Thinking that the two are talking about her, the girl starts feeling angry. She stops, walks back to the pair, and slugs the girl who was whispering. Having acted against her "antagonist," she continues down the hall.

It's a beautiful spring afternoon. Peter is contemplating skipping his geometry class and

heading to the park with his friends. Peter hates the class and is barely scraping by with a C. He can hardly wait until school's out and geometry is behind him. He thinks about sitting in the park with his friends. Then he thinks about sitting in class and trying to make sense of geometry. He really wants to skip, but he realizes that if he skips he'll just have to get notes from somebody in class and try to figure out the day's lesson on his own. That, Peter decides, is way too much trouble. He heaves a big sigh, then makes his way to class.

The three stories above illustrate only a few of the many ways that thoughts, feelings, and behaviors connect – and the different outcomes that are possible from those connections. In the first story, the student acknowledges the teacher's role in her life with positive thinking, feelings, and behavior.

But in the second story, negative thoughts and feelings spawn negative behavior.

And the third story is an example of how a student has negative feelings about geometry and contemplates a negative behavior (skipping class), but he is able to focus his thoughts and feelings and elect a positive behavior (attending class).

This interplay between thoughts, feelings, and behaviors is always with us. Our thoughts and feelings constantly influence our behavior – in good and bad ways. As adults, we usually do a pretty good job of keeping the outcome positive, but youth have a tougher time. Lacking life experience and its accompanying perspective, young people often make poor choices, particularly those youth who have come to rely on aggressive and violent behaviors to get their needs met.

In this chapter, we'll take a look at some of the components that make up thinking, feeling, and behaving, to explain what they are, what they mean as part of Conflict Cycles, and how students can learn to take control over them.

◆ Thinking

As human beings, we rely on our powers of thinking for nearly everything we do each day.

But sometimes – when we are frightened, for example – we tend to cast our powers of logic aside and just react. This is the famous "fight or flight" response, in which that chemical early warning device, adrenaline, rushes to our body's large muscle groups and readies us to do battle with an enemy or to run for our lives. When we are challenged like this, we usually don't stop to formulate an action plan – unless we have some type of training that helps us to focus on incorporating a thinking component into our reactions in situations like these.

This is what we need to teach our students. Much as police officers learn skills that help them make good decisions in dangerous situations, our kids can learn to react appropriately – and safely – in situations that challenge them.

◆ Building Blocks of Clear Thinking

The trick is to teach students HOW to think, not WHAT to think.

Knowing HOW to think includes these elements:

- Keeping your cool
- Sizing up the situation
- Thinking through the situation
- Doing the right thing

Here's a brief explanation of each of those elements:

▶ **Keeping your cool** – Faced with a challenging situation, many aggressive students' first reaction is to explode in anger. Their feelings boil over, and they lash out at the person who was unfortunate enough to be the bearer of bad news that day. These students react intensely to stressful situations. They take most things personally.

If the bus is late, for example, these students don't stop and think about perfectly neutral reasons such as a mechanical breakdown or the regular driver calling in sick. They also don't seem to realize that other people also are inconvenienced by the bus problem. Instead, they fume because the late bus has totally messed up their day, just like most other days get messed up. Nothing ever seems to go their way.

18

In order to keep their cool, these students need to learn that the world doesn't have a personal vendetta against them. And they need to learn some self-control methods that can help them manage their intense feelings when life throws them a curve ball.

We will discuss self-control methods later in this chapter. To work with students on the issue of taking everything personally, you may want to use the concepts described in the Corrective and Proactive Teaching chapters. Helping a student talk through a particular situation where he or she felt persecuted by events may be one way of teaching a more global view of the world.

▶ **Sizing up the situation** – As students learn to better control their anger and to view situations as more neutral than personal, they will gain more objectivity about the situations in which they find themselves.

You can help them size up situations by teaching them to look at the components of a situation such as antecedent, or precipitating, events and the people involved. Teach students to ask themselves what those involved may have to gain or lose by the outcome of the event and how those factors may motivate their actions. In addition, teach students to ask the same questions of themselves as they evaluate a situation. Usually, they will find that the event is not as earth-shattering as they originally thought.

▶ **Thinking through the situation** – After your students have grown accustomed to evaluating the separate components of a situation, they will have to learn how to put those pieces together and make decisions about potential outcomes. You will need to talk with your students about the best way to make those decisions, perhaps using the concept of "greatest

good" – maximum benefit to the greatest number of people – as a way to measure what should happen in a particular situation.

▶ **Doing the right thing** – This likely will be the most difficult step, as "the right thing" may be interpreted differently by different people. Again, the "greatest good" – maximum benefit to the greatest number of people – may be one defining principle in determining what is "the right thing."

If you can get students focused on the "greatest good," they can begin to see the world from another's perspective. This is the beginning of empathy and compassion – an important step for aggressive youth, who frequently lack skills to put themselves in someone else's shoes.

As students' moral values mature, they will be able to use their individual barometers to know how to solve problems. But learning what is right is going to be a lifelong process for most people. In the next section, we'll provide some specifics on how students can put their thinking skills to work in the problem-solving process.

◆ Thinking and Reasoning

Sometimes, students' thinking gets jumbled up when they use faulty reasoning to justify behavior. Some examples of that type of reasoning are outlined below (Peter, 1995; Halpern, 1996). When you hear students use these faulty reasons, point out the fallacies in their thinking. Use a series of structured questions, such as in Guided Self-Correction, to talk to them about the errors in their thinking, the effect their behavior has on others, and the effect others' behavior has on them. See Chapter 5 on Corrective Teaching for information about Guided Self-Correction.

Another way to teach youth to spot faulty reasoning is to have them use problem-solving strategies to dissect the bad logic in these statements. The more practice kids get in using independent thinking skills, the better.

◆ Faulty Reasoning

▶ **Intentional Exaggerations:** "Don't worry about your grades. You're good enough to play pro ball."

▶ **Believing Nonsense:** "I know I'm going to die young because the fortune teller at the circus said my lifeline is short."

▶ **Special Pleading:** The rules apply to everybody but you. "The cops never should have arrested us. We only took that car for 20 minutes, and we didn't trash it. We even parked it right back where it was parked before."

▶ **Ad Hominem Arguments:** You reject the argument because of the person. "I can't believe they let Maddie decide the prom theme. She hasn't had a date all year," or "Jeff says his friends weren't involved in the shooting, but you can't trust them because they're gangstas."

▶ **Genetic Fallacy:** You reject an argument based on a stereotype. "Anybody who would vote against open campus must be some kind of geek."

▶ **Appeal to Unqualified Authority:** Statements made by an uninformed person to purposefully mislead others. "Smoking isn't bad for you. There have been lots of studies to show that."

▶ **Appeal to Ignorance:** If you can't prove me wrong, then I must be right. "I'm not doing too good with my grades this semester, but it doesn't matter because I've already been accepted to Southern Cal."

▶ **Mob and Snob Appeal:** Groups and the media define what's best. "Why would you apply to colleges in town? Everybody goes as far away from home as possible for college!" or "Nike™ makes the best tennis shoes. Why would you buy any other brand?"

▶ **The Part for the Whole:** Some people are doing this; therefore everyone is. "My mom goes from one relationship to another. All women are like that."

▶ **Irrelevant Thesis:** A non-sequitur. "More kids are smoking these days. They should just let us smoke on campus so we don't have to sneak around."

▶ **Straw Man:** You make the issue seem unimportant to ease the pressure. "Why should I learn this stuff? I'm not going to college."

▶ **The Red Herring:** You use a diversionary tactic to ease the pressure. "Why are you getting on me about my homework? You never ask me one thing about cheerleading practice. You don't care at all about the things I like!"

You may want to develop a "Sponge Activity" in your classroom in which students make up their own versions of these fallacious reasonings or find examples of them in newspapers or magazines.

◆ Feelings

Think of how many feelings you experience each day. Maybe you're frustrated when you dribble coffee across the countertop as you sleepily pour that first cup of caffeine at the start of the day. Perhaps you're anxious as you sit in morning traffic and realize you're going to be late for work. You may feel overwhelmed when you see the pile of work on your desk. Maybe you're jealous when you hear about the colleague who won a weekend getaway by being the 25th caller to a radio drive-time show.

Some at-risk kids can't distinguish between such a variety of feelings. They may feel only mad, sad, bad, or glad. They haven't yet learned about nuances of feeling, so it's difficult for them to readily identify what emotions they are experiencing. Because of that, it also will be difficult for them to draw connections between their feelings and behaviors.

A student might insist, for example, that she was mad when she broke into tears during class, but maybe she was actually frustrated because she didn't understand the complicated math assignment you were explaining. After all, she's already struggling in your class.

You might have to gently explain that her behavior may be starting with frustration but escalating to anger by the time she recognizes it. Your job will be to teach her to recognize her frustration by learning to listen to her body. Does her stomach lurch when she's frustrated? Does her left eye twitch? Does she find herself making a fist?

After your student has learned to recognize the physical manifestations of her frustration, she must learn to develop an action plan to deal with it and keep it from escalating to anger. You can talk to her about using a self-control device

such as taking a break, getting a drink of water, etc., whatever it takes to rein in feelings before they give way to negative behaviors. But be patient. Allow some practice time and time for the student to grow comfortable with using these new techniques. Feelings are powerful and are not easily lassoed.

Remember that some aggressive students are harboring powerful feelings stemming from their life experiences. Some of their acting out can stem from those experiences. Keep in mind, though, that the hurt troubled students create may not be greater than the hurt they feel.

◆ Emotional Intelligence

Many aggressive and impulsive youth lack emotional intelligence, which is defined as the ability to monitor emotions and weigh alternatives before acting (Henley & Long, 1999).

These youth lack the ability to use reason and restraint when they find themselves in a stressful situation, and they also have difficulty understanding a situation from someone else's point of view. In addition, these students think little about the consequences of their actions (Henley & Long, 1999).

Youth without emotional intelligence tend to have these characteristics in common, according to Henley and Long:

- These students have little or no guilt about their behavior and therefore are not motivated to change it. They tend to use some fallacious reasoning, similar to those described earlier, including: assuming the role of the victim instead of the victimizer, rationalizing their behavior, or minimizing the conflict.

- They lack normal feelings of compassion toward others.

- They are self-centered, narcissistic, and rigidly proud.

- They believe personal aggression creates power and status.

In order to teach youngsters about emotional intelligence, you must focus on providing instruction in compassion and self-control, according to Henley and Long.

One way to teach compassion, they suggest, is to structure your classroom to run on cooperation rather than compliance and to emphasize the belief that students have the power within themselves to make needed changes.

Some teaching methods that encourage compassion and cooperation are: cooperative learning, brainstorming (which teaches students to listen and build on others' ideas), peer tutoring (lets students help others), role-playing (helps students see problems from different perspectives), and using literature written for young people (lets students begin to think through problems as they learn from role models in literature).

To teach students self-control, you may want to examine the self-control strategies in Chapter 10, as well as establish a classroom atmosphere that encourages students to be self-directed and to take responsibility for their own actions.

◆ Behaving

Behaviors are the most concrete clues we have to a student's thoughts and feelings. In many cases, they are good barometers to what those thoughts and feelings are, but in many other cases, a student's behavior may not be a good indication at all of what that youth is thinking or feeling.

In some cases, behaviors can be a visible indicator that a student either doesn't know what to do or has applied a behavior from another setting inappropriately. Watching a youth's behavior lets you know what that youth has learned and what needs to be reinforced.

Students must learn that their behavior affects others and that they can improve their chances for success by using behaviors that are pleasant and socially acceptable.

◆ Internalizing and Generalizing Behavior

As part of this process, students also must learn how to internalize and generalize the skills they learn.

Internalizing means that youth make new skills and behaviors a permanent part of their lives in order to be able to use them in the future. This usually has been accomplished when a student's thoughts and feelings reflect the teaching that has occurred. You can help your students internalize social skills by using Proactive Teaching (explained in Chapter 9 in this book), by practicing the skills and modeling them yourself in your classroom, and by actively teaching problem-solving.

Generalizing means that a student is able to use a skill or behavior in a variety of situations. This is where the "thinking" part of our three-pronged teaching approach comes into play. Kids who simply react to a situation, usually with inappropriate behavior, must learn how to sort through a situation and decide which skill or behavior will work best. This is a difficult step for kids whose needs have been ignored. But once a youth makes headway in this area, he or she has taken a big step toward taking responsibility and control in his or her life.

You can help your students generalize their life skills by giving them information about the different situations where a skill can be used and by role-playing some of those situations with students. You can use Proactive Teaching principles, giving youngsters "homework" to practice a skill in different settings, such as with a parent at home or with a friend in their neighborhood, and having them report the results the next day.

It is unreasonable to think that students are going to have positive thoughts, feelings, and behaviors in every situation. It is possible for a person to behave appropriately and still have negative thoughts and negative feelings about a situation. A person also could have positive thoughts and feelings and still fail to use right or socially acceptable behavior. For example, think about what kids experience when they skip school. They may feel scared that they'll get caught, but also joyful at the chance to escape for a bit.

In fact, many combinations of negative or positive thoughts, feelings, and behaviors are possible. This is especially true of teenagers, who often seem to be riding an emotional roller-coaster, with feelings that seem to be in permanent flux.

The point here is that you should not expect perfection from your students in the way they think, feel, or act. Rather, the goal should be to teach them how and why negative behaviors can harm them or cause them trouble and how using positive behaviors can benefit them or others. This teaching approach makes youth active participants in the learning process and prompts them to think and express their emotions.

Progress is measured by behavioral changes, but the student also is challenged to change on an intellectual and emotional level.

As students begin to make the links between their thoughts, feelings, and behaviors, they will be able to start identifying the negative thoughts and feelings that cause them to behave inappropriately – the triggers that launch their personal Conflict Cycles. Once students make those connections, they will be able to use the self-control skills offered in the following chapters to shape their behaviors, and, ultimately, the life choices they make.

Chapter Summary

Thinking
Building Blocks of Clear Thinking
    Keeping your cool
    Sizing up the situation
    Thinking through the situation
    Doing the right thing
Thinking and Reasoning
Faulty Reasoning

Feelings
Emotional Intelligence

Behaving
Internalizing and Generalizing Behavior

ChapterFive

Corrective Teaching

Tina Boyce's classroom was quiet on a Wednesday morning, as students used the first few minutes of the period to put final touches on their journal entries for the day. The English class was small – only five students – typical at the alternative high school that served the large urban district.

Ms. Boyce was a tall, no-nonsense woman who appeared intimidating at first because of her straightforward manner, but she forged strong relationships with her students. She loved teaching and cared deeply about her students, and they responded well to her. Because of that, she was able to be very candid with the youngsters, talking with them openly about her high expectations for them.

Ms. Boyce did a lot of one-on-one teaching with the students, and this morning was no exception. She made her rounds, spending time with each student discussing individual assignments. Each of the students was fulfilling different requirements, but each was required to turn in a journal entry every morning.

The teacher stopped by Aaron's desk to check his journal. The sophomore handed her his notebook, and she began to read as he stashed away a sheaf of papers and started doodling on the front cover of another notebook.

"What's this?" she asked him incredulously, with a slight twinkle in her eye. "I saw this yesterday. You changed the date and now you're trying to tell me this is what you wrote today?

"Oh no," Ms. Boyce said firmly. Then she bent down, putting her face close to Aaron's. Chuckling, she said, "No way. You can't fool me. When are you going to learn that there is NO WAY you can pull the wool over my eyes? I know ALL the tricks."

Aaron stared down at his doodles and shifted a bit in his seat as Ms. Boyce stepped back and dropped the journal unceremoniously on his desk. When the falling journal landed on the desk, it dislodged the pile of papers, which scattered to the floor. The teacher kept talking, focusing on the student rather than the scattered papers.

"I'm disappointed that you have so little respect for me that you thought you could deceive me," the teacher told Aaron. "And I'm disappointed that you care so little about your grade that you would risk getting a zero today. Do you want a zero?"

"No, ma'am," Aaron said, shyly looking up at his teacher. "I'm sorry."

"I accept your apology. Thank you. Now here's a deal. You have 15 minutes to write up your journal entry for today. That means a new entry with today's date."

Then, the teacher bent to pick up the fallen papers and began handing them to Aaron. The writing on one caught her attention.

"What's this?" she asked Aaron. The paper bore a note that Aaron was writing to a boy named Roberto, who was called "Berto." In the note, Aaron told Berto that he'd heard that two other students – Kevin and Shawn – were responsible for stealing Berto's boombox from his car.

"What are you trying to do with this note?" Ms. Boyce said, her voice all business. "This kind of note gets fights started. You KNOW that. You would not be a responsible person if you gave Berto this note, no matter how good a friend you think you're being. Now tear it up."

Ms. Boyce stood over Aaron as he tore up the note. She stood for a moment, not saying anything. Then she reached for the wastebasket and watched as he dropped the pieces of the note in the trash. The teacher spoke to the student then, her voice slightly softer than it had been a moment earlier. "Do you understand why it's wrong to pass along gossip? Do you know how it can hurt people?"

Aaron was staring down at his desk now, not daring to look up at the teacher. He nodded "yes" silently, then stole a glance as Ms. Boyce replaced the wastebasket in the corner.

"Aaron, I know you're smart, and you know what it means to do the right thing. You've handled a lot of tough criticism this morning. I'm going to give you the opportunity to get back to work on your journal now. But you'll need to see me at the end of the day to finish it. We can talk more about this then."

"Yes, ma'am."

When students make poor choices, you have an opportunity to teach them to make better choices the next time. That's the concept behind the Boys Town teaching method called **Corrective Teaching**, a systematic approach that you can use to identify children's inappropriate behavior and guide them toward appropriate behavior.

Corrective Teaching has three central concepts: Description, Relationship, and Consequence.

▶ **The Description** concept includes describing a behavior in words or actions, role-playing, and practice.

▶ **The Relationship** concept involves using friendliness and warmth and showing genuine concern for the youth. It also involves helping the child to feel good about himself or herself. More information about forging relationships with students can be found in Chapter 7.

▶ **The Consequence** concept includes praise, feedback, and, obviously, a consequence for the inappropriate behavior. We will discuss more about consequences later in this chapter.

Effective teaching requires a balance among the Description, Relationship, and Consequence concepts.

Corrective Teaching works best when students are making mistakes and don't know how to correct them. You can use Corrective Teaching for both academic and social skills deficits. A few examples of social skills deficits that can be addressed by Corrective Teaching include not following instructions or having difficulty accepting feedback from others.

As you can see, a number of these situations relate directly to behaviors that could quickly escalate into aggression. Corrective Teaching gives you a structured, yet flexible plan for dealing with many kinds of inappropriate behaviors. The teaching method allows you to deal consistently with students and provides young people the opportunity to learn positive ways to get what they want or to settle their differences with others. The key to successful Corrective Teaching is developing solid relationships with your students.

How does Corrective Teaching work? The scenario earlier is an example, and the scenario below is broken down into its component parts to show how the teaching might sound. In this example, the teacher is talking to Amy, who is disappointed because she received a C on a paper the teacher just returned. Notice the use of the essential Description, Relationship, and Consequence components.

▶**Initial praise/empathy:** "I know it can be frustrating when you do not get the grade you want."

▶**Describe inappropriate behavior:** "When you wrote this paragraph, you had a lot of run-on sentences. You combined too many ideas or phrases in one sentence. You wrote 'When my parents left me alone for the first time, I was excited about having the whole house to myself, but after a short time the sounds of the night made me uneasy because I never really noticed them before.' "

▶**Describe appropriate behavior:** "After you write something, read it aloud. If you pause or hesitate at a certain point, you need to insert a comma, a semicolon, or a period. Don't overuse connect words like 'but' or 'because.' Watch for changes in the topic covered in the sentence. When you change the topic, start a new sentence. If you have more than 20 words in a sentence, check it carefully to make sure it's not a run-on sentence. Eliminate any unnecessary words or phrases."

▶**Give a rationale:** "When you avoid run-on sentences, your papers will probably be easier to read. You'll convey your wonderful thoughts better."

▶**Request acknowledgment:** "Okay, does that make sense? Do you have any questions?"

▶**Practice:** "Please rewrite this paragraph and check back with me when you've finished."

▶**Feedback:** "Nice job of rewriting. You avoided those run-on sentences we talked about. Good work!"

▶**Consequence:** "By correcting your work, you ensured a B on your paper."

▶**General praise:** "I knew you could do it!"

Let your students' behaviors guide you in how you conduct Corrective Teaching. Usually, their behaviors will give you clues about what they need, and you can target those needs when you talk to students about their behaviors. For example, a student who talks back to you may be seeking attention, so your Corrective Teaching will sound different from how it is used with a youngster who needs direction on how to show an algebra proof.

With the hectic pace of most classrooms, you may find it difficult to find the time to always use all the steps outlined earlier. The good news is, you don't have to. Because the Boys Town Teaching Model is extremely flexible, you can do Corrective Teaching in as few as two steps, particularly with students with whom you have strong relationships and students who are familiar with the teaching. Younger children also will respond more favorably to teaching that is less complex.

In the earlier story about Tina Boyce and Aaron, the teacher used shorter variations of Corrective Teaching.

In her first discussion with the boy, the teacher discussed Aaron's attempt to pass off an earlier journal entry as today's entry. Ms. Boyce described the student's inappropriate behavior and gave him an opportunity to correct his behavior by creating a current journal entry in 15 minutes. He also received a consequence of meeting with the teacher after school.

In this example, the teacher had developed a solid relationship with the student, so, for him, it also was a significant consequence when the teacher expressed her disappointment in him.

In her second Corrective Teaching, Ms. Boyce described the student's other poor behavior choice in writing the letter to his friend about the stolen boombox. She explained to him how the letter might cause a fight, and she issued a consequence by having him tear up the letter.

As you do Corrective Teaching, remember that it's important to reinforce your relationship with the student at the same time you are correcting him or her. Using your voice tone and word choice, communicate to the student that all is not lost, that he or she can correct the problem behavior and move on to other successes. Remain positive. Let the student know that your current disappointment won't cloud your future relationship with the youngster.

You might want to use a **positive correction** statement when you talk to the student. A positive correction statement acknowledges the consequence the student has earned, but adds some hope. It sounds like this: "Jamie, you'll need to come in and see me after school, but you'll be able to leave as soon as you finish those math problems."

After you become familiar with the basics of Corrective Teaching, you will be able to use the shorter variations. There are a variety of situations where you would use these variations, including with students with whom you have a strong relationship and who can accept consequences without praise or empathy. You also can use these variations in situations where students understand how to change their behaviors, as well as those where a student needs a consequence to understand and learn a skill. As you become more skilled at Corrective Teaching, you will be able to create your own variations.

◆ Corrective Teaching Variations

▶ **Two-Step – Consequence & Practice or Positive Correction:** "You didn't show your work on your math problems, so your grade is a D, but if you fix the problems by sixth period and bring them back in, you can bump the grade up to a C."

▶ **Three-Step – Description of Inappropriate, Description of Appropriate, Consequence:** "You blurted out a question in class instead of raising your hand and waiting for me to acknowledge you first. Now, you'll have to wait until I answer questions from students who waited to be called on."

▶ **Four Step – Empathy, Consequence, Description of Inappropriate, Practice or Positive Correction:** "I realize it's frustrating to have your project fail. It looks like you skipped a step. You forgot to add the solution it calls for in Step 3, so you didn't get the bubbles you were supposed to get. Why don't you start over and I'll be back to help you."

Remember, these variations are effective when you: 1) have a good relationship with the student; 2) have practiced these variations beforehand and feel comfortable using them, and 3) do not overuse these techniques.

◆ Guided Self-Correction

"Matt, your homeroom teacher told me that he counted you as absent yesterday when you were running that errand for me. How do you think you can fix that so you won't have an unexcused absence?"

"I guess I should get a pass from you. I didn't think about that yesterday."

"Good thinking. Why do you think it's important to plan ahead and get a pass?"

"So I won't have an absence, and people will know where I went."

"Great! Here's the pass. I'll give you a few minutes to run this down to the office and explain the situation to them."

"Thanks. I won't forget next time."

Bryce has been teasing another student in his middle school homeroom class by imitating the Sesame Street character Big Bird whenever he sees the other youngster, whose name is Sam

Byrd. Bryce's comments belittle Sam. So far, Sam has ignored Bryce.

One day before class starts, Bryce leans back in his chair and starts making comments about Sam just now learning the alphabet. As he walks past Bryce, Sam wheels around and pushes Bryce's chair, which tips over backwards, sending Bryce into a tumble.

Bryce starts to go after Sam, but their teacher, Ed Robertson, steps between the two boys. Mr. Robertson orders Sam to his seat, then pulls Bryce aside in the back of the room.

"Help me understand what just happened, Bryce?"

"I don't know. I was just sitting there and Big Byrd knocked the chair out from under me?"

"Are you sure nothing else happened?"

Bryce thinks for a minute, then looks sheepishly down at the floor. "Well, he might not have liked being called Big Byrd."

"Maybe not. Can you see where you might have provoked him?"

"I guess so."

"How would you feel if somebody made fun of your name? Would you be mad?"

"I guess so."

"Okay. You wouldn't like to be called a name, so you know Sam's not enjoying it either. What can you do to make things better between you and Sam?"

"I can say I'm sorry."

"That's good clear thinking, Bryce. I appreciate you taking time to see how your actions might hurt other people. I hope you'll think about that the next time you're tempted to tease someone. You know what? We've got a few minutes before the bell rings, so this may be a good time to make that apology. What do you think?"

"Okay, Mr. Robertson."
"Good job, Bryce."

These scenarios are examples of Guided Self-Correction, a variation of Corrective Teaching that uses a series of questions to guide a student through the teaching process.

Guided Self-Correction encourages students to be more active participants in the learning process by helping them think about the situation and determine why they're being corrected. By answering the questions, the students can demonstrate that they know what they did wrong and can use problem-solving skills to correct the situation.

Guided Self-Correction is especially effective with older students because it challenges them to be accountable and to solve problems for themselves.

You can use questions such as these in Guided Self-Correction: "Help me understand what just happened here?"; "What can you do now?"; "What did you do that got bad results?"; "How can you fix it?"; "How can I help?"

The first question you ask is usually very general and is conveyed in a nonthreatening manner, such as "Talk to me about what happened here." The point of this basic question is to lay a foundation for the more specific questions that you'll ask later.

By asking "What happened?", you ask students to describe the situation in which they find themselves. Essentially, you are asking them to take the first step toward recognizing they did something wrong, but your tone is not accusatory. You simply ask students to describe the situation in an effort to get them to see their role in it.

The next few questions are more specific, dealing with the nuts and bolts of the situation. You ask questions like: "Why do you think he got mad?"; "What would you have done if you were in his position?"; "What can you do now that might make things better?"; "What would be a positive solution to this problem?"

With these questions, you are guiding students toward a solution to the problem and an understanding of their part in the situation, as well as an opportunity to "walk in somebody else's shoes."

When you help students to see the connections between their behaviors and the situations they find themselves in, they begin to realize that they have the power to solve their own problems and will want to apply their ideas to other settings. Students become self-directed, taking ownership of their actions, and being accountable for their behaviors. As they grow comfortable with their new responsibility, they will be reinforced by the chance to use their decision-making skills.

Keep in mind that using Guided Self-Correction is a gradual process and that you may have to prompt students along the way to keep them aware of how their behavior can result in consequences for them. For example, in the story about Bryce and Sam, it might have been necessary for the teacher to point out to Bryce that Sam got mad because Bryce called him "Big Byrd," if Bryce wasn't making the connection between the two events. Then, the teacher could help Bryce make more connections by asking questions about Bryce's actions and Sam's responses.

◆ Consequences

Consequences are part of life. When children are young, they learn that they'll get burned if they touch a hot stove or earn a time-out for stealing a little brother's toy. As children, fear of consequences like these may keep them walking the straight-and-narrow path of good behavior.

But as children grow older, their expanding life experiences expose them to many consequences, as well as inconsistent enforcement of consequences. Those experiences may make them blasé about what impact consequences can have on their lives.

By the time youngsters are in their teen years, then, many are pretty oblivious to consequences. Yes, they're probably familiar with the laundry list of rules that constitute consequences in their school districts, but most will tell you that they are more motivated by what their friends are doing than by what district policy says is the right thing to do.

So how can you make consequences meaningful as part of Corrective Teaching with students?

Two concepts are essential: teaching the idea of community and consistent enforcement.

The idea of community is that students are part of a community in school. When someone participates in an activity – like acting out in a classroom, for example – that disrupts other members of the community, that student has violated a bond of trust between students in the community. If students learn to see themselves as socially responsible members of the school community, they will not want to disappoint other members of that community by acting in a way that earns them a consequence. Social skills instruction will help students learn ways to get their needs met without having to violate the needs of other students in the classroom.

The second concept, consistent enforcement of consequences, is essential to safely governing a school. If the rules change every day, they no longer have any impact, and students start ignoring them. Administrators and teachers must be consistent about leveling consequences; they shouldn't "wink" at an infraction by a student athlete, then lower the boom on the junior with green spiked hair. By showing your students that everyone is treated equally, you send a message that you're serious about the rules you make and that those rules form the foundation for your school as a community.

Chapter Summary

Corrective Teaching: A teaching process that you can use to identify inappropriate behavior in students and guide them toward appropriate behavior. The central concepts of Corrective Teaching are: Description, Relationship, and Consequence.

Description: Describing behavior in words or actions, role-playing and practice

Relationship: Using friendliness and warmth; showing genuine concern for student; helping student feel good about himself

Consequence: Praise, feedback, and a consequence for inappropriate behavior

Using Corrective Teaching

When students are making mistakes and don't know how to correct them

Use with both social skills and academic deficits

Use to defuse aggressive behaviors

Step-by-Step

Initial praise/empathy

Describe inappropriate behavior

Describe appropriate behavior

Give a rationale

Request acknowledgment

Practice

Feedback

Consequence

General praise

Variations

Guided Self-Correction: A variation of Corrective Teaching that uses a series of questions to guide a student through the teaching process

Consequences

Students as members of a community

Consistent enforcement

Chapter Six

Crisis Teaching

Morning math class is about to begin, and teacher Bruce Jones is watching two students, Jim Randolph and Marquis Abbott, glare at one another. When the two entered the classroom a few minutes ago, Marquis was saying, "You ain't hard, punk," to Jim in a loud, angry voice. Jim responded, "We'll see about that, you little 'ho."

Mr. Jones knows there's bad blood between the two boys. Jim, a new student who already has established himself as a discipline problem, is a loud, aggressive youth who makes no secret of the fact that he dislikes Marquis. A tackle on the football team, Jim tends to pick fights and then pretend not to understand when another student lashes out at him.

Marquis has been working on controlling his temper because he has had several office referrals for fighting in school this semester. He is trying hard to do what's right, Mr. Jones believes.

The teacher intervenes by telling both boys to quiet down and take their seats for class. He tells them that he'll be speaking with them after he finishes returning their quizzes.

As the teacher moves around the classroom returning the quizzes, he sees Jim turning around in his seat glaring at Marquis. Marquis is trying to ignore him. Mr. Jones says to Jim: "Jim, could you please face the front? I'll be right with you."

When Mr. Jones returns Jim's quiz, he stops in front of the student's desk and says, "Jim, I noticed you staring back and the comments you made earlier. Is there a problem? Otherwise our priority is algebra, and we need to get to work. We'll talk more a little later."

Jim looks up at the teacher with a blank look in his eyes, then turns back toward Marquis and says angrily, "Ain't you gonna say somethin' to his punk a--?"

Marquis jumps out of his seat, his eyes flashing. "What you want, Waterboy? You keep talking loud, but everybody knows you soft."

"F--- you! How's that?" screams Jim, jumping out of his seat.

"Okay, Jim, Marquis. It stops here," Mr. Jones says. "Take your seats NOW."

Marquis sits down, but Jim remains standing. The teacher senses that Jim enjoys having the whole class watching him.

"Jim, here's the deal. You can choose to make things worse for yourself, or you can take a seat and we can work this out," the teacher says.

"Work what out? A f------ detention?" Jim asks, in a slightly lower but still agitated tone as he plops angrily into his seat.

"Thanks for sitting down, Jim. You made a good decision. We'll talk in a few minutes. Why don't you take a minute now and chill? No business is going to be handled in here anyway."

"Okay, everybody," Mr. Jones says addressing the class. "Thanks for minding your business right now. I want you to break up into your groups and work on your research projects. I'll be around to check with each group in a few minutes."

As the students gather in their research groups, the teacher motions Jim aside and says, "Thanks for giving me some time to get the class organized. Now what's up with all this drama?"

"What do you care?" says Jim, with the sarcasm heavy in his voice. "Just write me up so I can get this over with. I got a job so I can't be here after school."

"I'm not writing you up. You're calming down. How about this? Let's visit during the last few minutes of class about what happened. Can you get through the rest of the class this morning?"

"Yeah, I guess so, as long as your pet don't talk no stuff."

"First, I have no pets except my dog Justice at home. I'm going to speak with Marquis, then we'll get together those last five minutes, okay?"

"Yeah, I'm cool," Jim says with an air of resignation.

During the last few minutes of class, while the other students are finishing up their group discussions and waiting for the bell, the teacher sits down with Jim.

"Jim, you did a good job of calming down this morning. Are you still cool or do you need to talk some more?"

"I'm cool. What's up?"

"Well, we need to talk about the consequences for cursing when you got angry. Talk to me about what happened with Marquis."

The student sighs. "He's a trip, man. I think he and his gangsta wannabes are gonna be comin' for me, so I just wanna be ready. Back where I come from you always gotta watch your back. I'm about it."

The teacher is incredulous. "You think Marquis is in a gang?"

"Yeah," the student says ."That's what I heard."

"Well, you heard wrong. Marquis' brother was in a gang; he got shot and killed last year. Marquis won't have anything to do with gangs. You got yourself some bad information, Jim. The only reason it feels like this is because being kinda new, you're just trying to let them know you aren't a punk and guess what? They feel the same way. You all have more in common than you think."

The student looks down at the floor, embarrassed, not wanting to face the teacher.

"Now, what do you think you can do to make things better with Marquis?" Mr. Jones asks.

"Well, if he ain't no gang banger, that's cool. I don't want no drama with him or his boys, but I'm not going out like a sucker," says Jim.

"That's right. I can admire that. What can we do?"

"I don't know. I'll just back off. You want me to apologize or something?"

"That would make things right, Jim. Give it some thought, okay? I'd also like to get you together man to man and squash this. Just you two and me. Now let's talk about cursing. When you get mad, what would be a better choice than cursing? Can you think of a way you could calm down and not earn a consequence for your behavior?" the teacher asks.

"I could ask to be excused or I could just chill," Jim says.

"That's good clear thinking, Jim. Will you try that next time?"

"I'll give it a shot," the student says.

"Great! Now we've got to talk about consequences. Since you're trying to be a man and stand up for yourself, I want you to know that a real man takes responsibility for his consequences. All right? You know cursing earns you a detention, but I know you have a job after school, so I'm going to give you a choice of a before-school detention so you can still get to work. You'll have to do 30 minutes one morning this week starting at 7:30. What day will you be in?"

Jim sighs. "I guess Wednesday. I can catch a ride with my mom that day."

"Okay, Wednesday it is. I'll tell the office to expect you in morning detention that day. Thanks for sitting here and talking this through calmly with me. And think about those choices you can make to control your anger, okay? When I get with Marquis, we'll look at hooking you two up together and talking about what's happening for real. Cool?"

"Cool, Mr. Jones."

"Thanks, Jim."

It's first period Art class and Terri James, a sophomore, is late for the third time this week. Her teacher, Betty West, meets her at the door.

"Terri, you're late again. Do you have a pass?"

"Nope. If I did, wouldn't I be showing you?" the student says flippantly.

"And what have I told you about getting a pass?"

"I'm sorry. Damn. I'll go get a pass," Terri says, her voice agitated.

"And when you get back, we'll discuss the detention you're getting for being late so much," the teacher says.

"You don't have to get smart. I said I was sorry. I won't get the pass if you keep popping off."

"Now you're being sarcastic. You really need to work on your attitude, young lady," says Ms. West.

"You're the one. I apologized and you keep dissin' me," Terri says, frustrated. "Whatever," she adds, starting to leave.

"If you walk out of here now, you'll get an F for the day and, believe me, you cannot afford that," the teacher says with an edge in her voice.

"I don't care. I'm transferring out of this class. So you know what you can do with your F."

"Well, you make that choice. And I do know – mark it in the grade book."

"Whatever – that's why nobody can't stand your a--." With that, the student turns from the teacher and walks out of the classroom, slamming the door on the way.

Many troubled kids like Jim and Terri make unhealthy choices when they lose self-control in times of conflict or crisis. While most people successfully deal with these conflict and crisis situations on a daily basis, kids who lack the key skills necessary to control their own behaviors during times of emotional distress many times respond with aggressive or negative behavior. This keeps them from successfully resolving conflicts and leads to many negative consequences.

How do we reach kids like these and help them learn the skills of self-control? At Boys Town, we've learned that the ability to make good decisions in emotionally charged settings is a key to maintaining healthy relationships. To assist children toward reaching this goal, we use a method called Crisis Teaching.

Jim's teacher successfully used the tools of Crisis Teaching to help Jim realize that angry responses in class aren't productive, but Terri's teacher lost her own self-control and got into an argument with the student, resulting in a negative outcome.

The goal of Crisis Teaching is to help students regain self-control and give them skills so they can manage their responses the next time. Kids who can face adverse situations without using negative or hurtful behaviors are more capable of getting their needs met, and are better able to cope with stress, positively change their behaviors, and successfully resolve conflicts.

By using these self-control skills, kids are able to stop their usual negative responses, think of alternative ways of coping, and choose better ways of dealing with what can seem like insurmountable dilemmas. Teaching youth to use self-control strategies helps them begin to assume responsibility for changing their own antisocial behavior in ways that produce constructive and long-lasting results.

◆ Crisis Teaching: A Step-by-Step Look

Crisis Teaching in the classroom is challenging because you must balance the needs of a youngster who is upset and uncooperative with your responsibility to teach your other students. Your goal is to restore order to the classroom and teach the disruptive student self-control, along with some appropriate behaviors they can use to get their needs met. As with all Teaching Interactions, keep in mind that the stronger your relationships are with your students, the more successful results you'll have.

Crisis Teaching has four components:
1. **Address the problem behavior.**
2. **Monitor your self-control.**
3. **Ensure student self-control.**
4. **Engage student in follow-up teaching or problem-solving.**

Here's a look at each of the components:

▶ **Address the problem behavior:** In the situation with Jim, the teacher addressed the problem behavior of cursing by reminding the student what he should be doing – "Jim, this morning our priority is algebra."

Then, the teacher gave Jim an instruction: "Please turn around and face forward." By setting an expectation, a teacher can find out if a student is under self-control. Jim had difficulty following the instruction, so the teacher knew more teaching was necessary. If Jim had been able to follow the instruction, the teacher may have been able to do Corrective Teaching rather than Crisis Teaching.

If the student is engaging in physical behavior that could harm himself or others, it should be stopped immediately. You can first use a firm instruction to tell the child to stop, but if the behavior is serious and dangerous (punching, kicking, hitting someone with an object, etc.), you may have to intervene physically. If you intervene, you should act quickly and use only as much physical force as necessary. Keep in mind that your district policy may prohibit some types of physical intervention.

If you do intervene, your action may be simple, such as putting a firm hand on the shoulder of a boy to stop him from throwing a punch. Or you might find yourself in a more volatile setting, such as talking a girl into handing over a pocketknife that she's using to threaten a classmate. Be sure to ask for help if the situation is one you can't handle safely by yourself.

▶ **Monitor your self-control:** This component is crucial because you cannot help the student regain his or her self-control if you are not in control of your own behavior. When you monitor your self-control, you tune in to how you are communicating. You keep your voice low and even. You praise students for calming down or make empathy statements to show you understand they're having difficulty.

And it's also important to NOT let yourself get drawn into an argument with the student. If you do, you'll end up like the teacher in the second example, matching the student in witty and not-so-witty retorts and eventually spiraling downward into an outcome that benefits no one. Remember: It's extremely easy to become sarcastic and condescending with a student if you get drawn into an argument.

One way to avoid being drawn into an argument is to think of yourself as a video camera. Your job is to view and neutrally describe what the student's behavior is. You might say, for example, "Shante, you're walking around. How about taking a seat?"

If you find yourself losing self-control, it's a good idea to suggest that the student take a few minutes to calm down. Then you can spend a few minutes away from the student regaining your self-control too.

Let's go back to the first example in this chapter, where Jim earned a detention for cursing. What if a student loudly cursed at you? How would you keep your self-control in the face of angry epithets?

If your school's discipline code says that cursing is an automatic office referral, then you could use the code as a matter-of-fact way to respond to the cursing. You'd simply tell the student that he or she has violated the code and must report to the office.

Or, if your school district code gives you some leeway when a student curses, you may choose to handle the matter without referring the student to the office. If you make that choice, you'll want to ask yourself a variety of questions: Can you stay calm, cool and collected when you deal with a cursing student, or is cursing one of your hot buttons? Can the action you take in the classroom to end the cursing benefit the student? Do you have a strong enough relationship with the student to handle this volatile situation? How will this situation affect your other students?

▶ **Ensure student self-control:** After you make certain that your behavior is under control, you can start working with the student to help him or her regain control.

In the first scenario, teacher Bruce Jones used a combination of empathy and praise statements to help calm Jim. In addition, the teacher reminded the student, "You can choose to make things worse for yourself, or you can take a seat and we can work this out."

The teacher also gave Jim a few minutes to calm himself and then checked with the student to see if he was able to maintain his calm demeanor. If you have worked with students previously to develop self-control strategies, such as taking deep breaths, you can remind them to start using them. The strategies are explained in more detail later in this book.

If you have not worked with students to help them develop self-control strategies, you can begin this process when you do follow-up teaching or problem-solving with the student. Then, you can use Proactive Teaching to help students learn those skills.

▶ **Engage student in follow-up teaching or problem-solving:** When your student has regained self-control, you will be able to talk with him or her about the behavior, describing briefly why it is inappropriate, and about making a better choice next time.

In addition, you can help students choose strategies to help them in the future. In the first scenario, for example, the teacher did follow-up teaching with Jim about ways to control his anger. One of the best ways to do this is to engage the student in the process by asking him or her a question. For example, the teacher asked Jim, "Can you think of a way you could calm down and not earn a consequence for your behavior?"

This component of Crisis Teaching also includes giving a consequence, which lets students know that you are serious about helping them change their behaviors. They begin to understand that they have to pay a price for losing self-control. If possible, tie the consequence to the misbehavior so youngsters can see the connection between their behavior and how it impacts not only their lives but others' lives.

◆ Benefits of Crisis Teaching

Crisis Teaching provides you with a reliable, structured teaching system to use in the very worst teaching environment – when a youth is in crisis.

This teaching system gives you techniques to calm the troubled student and helps you teach the student self-control strategies that he or she can use in the future.

The structure helps you focus your teaching so you don't get caught up in arguing with the student, possibly escalating the situation, and damaging the relationship you've built with the youngster. The format of Crisis Teaching helps you focus on the student's behavior of talking or arguing, rather than on the words that are being said, so you don't get drawn into the crisis.

◆ How to Use Crisis Teaching

Here are some tips for using Crisis Teaching:

▶ **Stay calm.** Your ability to stay calm will determine whether Crisis Teaching works. If your student is angry or upset and you get angry or upset, you risk escalating the situation. It is vital that you train yourself not to let anything your students say or do make you lose self-control. Remaining relaxed and calm also models the behaviors you want your students to use and lets them know that you are serious about teaching new behaviors.

▶ **Be aware of your physical actions.** While teaching, your physical actions are as important as what you say and how you say it. Using behaviors that your student might interpret as being aggressive or threatening may only serve to make a bad situation even worse. These behaviors might include "stalking" or shadowing the student if he or she leaves the room, using a harsh or demanding voice, standing over a child to establish your "dominance," pointing your index finger, standing with your hands on your hips, raising a fist, or putting your face close to the student's face. All these gestures set the stage for confrontation rather than conversation.

Sitting down, being at eye level with a student, and keeping your hands relaxed or in pockets or your arms at your sides helps avoid these negative gestures and others that might seem intimidating. Another calming method that works is deep-breathing.

▶ **Be patient.** Learning self-control can take a long time. So don't expect too much too soon, and don't be disappointed when your students don't show improvement as quickly as you'd like. Pay attention to small victories, and heap praise on students for even the smallest progress. Above all, don't give up. The stakes for your students, and for you, are much too high.

◆ When to Use Crisis Teaching

Sometimes, teachers overreact to students' behaviors and jump into Crisis Teaching too quickly. If this happens a lot, a student might start thinking that you are going to make a federal case out of even the most minor misbehavior. This is not a healthy classroom situation. It's usually best to consider whether Corrective Teaching will do the job when a misbehavior occurs. If the negative behavior continues or is so extreme that you have no other choice, then start Crisis Teaching.

There also will be times when teaching is not the answer. Sometimes, kids get so overwhelmed or confused by their emotions that they just need someone to listen. Simply asking a child if there's a problem and telling him or her

that you're there to help can sometimes prevent or calm a potentially volatile situation. For example, say something like "I know you're upset. If you can calm down, we can talk about it." The more you teach and the more your students learn, the easier it should be for you to decide whether to use Crisis Teaching or some other intervention.

◆ Relationship Components of Crisis Teaching

We've talked at length about using the Boys Town Teaching Model as a classroom management tool. Now, we'll offer some other suggestions – what we call quality components – that enhance teaching. These suggestions will help you manage your own behavior and de-escalate confrontations with aggressive or violent students.

It isn't always easy to stay calm when a youth is yelling, making threats, calling you names, or refusing to follow instructions. Your first inclination will be to respond emotionally to these actions, rather than focusing on teaching to the youth's problem behaviors.

But if the goal of teaching during a crisis situation is for a child to learn self-control, it is essential for you to model self-control. The following sections explain some of the important physical and emotional elements – relationship components – that should be present when you work with youth who have lost self-control. Ideally, these components will be present in all your teaching.

▶ **Offer the youth "cool-down" time.** Offering students a chance to cool down is an excellent strategy for successfully managing a crisis, and may be used at other times when youngsters are upset or frustrated. Taking a few minutes to regroup may mean the situation doesn't escalate into a crisis. "Cool-down" time is an opportunity for you to regain your composure while the student uses self-control strategies to calm down.

▶ **Spend time telling the child what he or she is doing right.** When a crisis occurs, adults tend to focus on what youngsters are doing wrong. It is easy to deal with these negative behaviors because they are visible, obvious, and sometimes "in your face."

When we focus on these behaviors, we often say things like "You need to change your attitude" or "Straighten up your act." Besides being perceived as negative, these statements are extremely vague. They don't give the student specific information about what needs to be corrected.

Instead, you can make statements such as "Please stop pacing" or "You are glaring at me." Try to make these statements in a calm fashion. This accomplishes two things: It gives the student specific information about what he or she is doing wrong, and it gives you something to focus on so you won't be drawn into an argument with the student.

In addition, you should start looking for positive behaviors to praise. For example, if the student has been pacing and sits down, you could say "Nice job of sitting down, Jim. You made a good decision to stop pacing" or "Thanks for looking at me so calmly and not glaring."

Spending time telling the youth what he or she is doing right will have a tremendous effect on your outlook during this stressful time. It will help you remain upbeat, positive, and calm.

▶ **Talk softly and slowly.** The tone and volume of your voice can have a big impact on how a student in crisis responds to you. Talking loudly or shouting can make a teenager think that you are yelling at him or her, while talking fast only confuses the youth. This is a bad combination and will surely escalate a crisis situation.

As you concentrate on lowering your voice and talking more slowly, you begin to calm down. When you sound calm, you model how you want your student to speak. This is a big step toward resolving a crisis situation more quickly, because such modeling can soften the intensity of a child's inappropriate behaviors and head off further escalation.

▶ **Remain relaxed.** Be aware of behaviors like clenching your fists, glaring at the child, pounding your hand on the table, towering over a student, or crossing your arms. A youth is likely to perceive these kinds of actions as aggressive or threatening, and this will escalate the situation. One excellent method for calming yourself physically is to take a deep breath and let the air out slowly. Do this several times. This is an easy relaxation procedure that can be done quickly and almost anywhere. Your body will become less tense, and you will regain your composure.

▶ **Avoid arguing.** In a crisis, some kids are masters at dragging adults into arguments and debates about issues that have nothing to do with the problem at hand. Their goal is to move away from the issue so that you will forget about the current difficulties they are having and the negative consequences they will earn. The next thing you know, you are debating the fairness of a detention the student earned two weeks ago or defending yourself against accusations that you play favorites in the classroom.

Usually, this is a smoke screen that has helped the youth stay out of trouble in the past. The point is that when you get caught up in these trivial arguments and debates, you'll not only lose, but also become more frustrated and angry.

In these situations, you can keep your cool by letting the student know that you understand that he or she has some issues to discuss and that you would be willing to discuss them once the youth has calmed down and worked through the present problem. In this way, you demonstrate that you respect what the student has to say and you remain calm while avoiding a fruitless debate.

Avoiding these debates is a good rule of thumb. But, like any rule, there are exceptions. There will be times when immediately listening to what a youngster has to say can help solve a crisis. If a student uncharacteristically becomes teary-eyed and begins sobbing, find out what's wrong.

This should give you a better understanding of why the youth is upset and the reason for the negative behaviors. You also are showing genuine concern, which goes a long way in strengthening your relationship with the student.

This is an excellent opportunity to spend some time talking through the problem with the student and helping him or her find a solution. Later, once the intense emotions have subsided, you can return to the original issue and teach the youth a better way to deal with a problem.

A word of caution: Some youngsters learn to automatically turn on the tears at the first sign of trouble. This behavior may have allowed them to escape negative consequences in the past. When deciding whether to discuss an issue during a crisis situation, you will have to rely on your expertise and judgment. There is no tried-and-true formula to tell you when it is right or wrong. The key is to know the youth you are working with and to be sure that the behavior is one you don't normally see from that student.

▶ **Watch your words.** Don't say things that "put down" your students. Comments such as "You'll never learn anything!" or "We've gone over this a thousand times!" serve only to escalate a crisis and ruin relationships.

Also, the manner in which you speak can send harmful messages to students. When you use a condescending or smug voice, even a positive statement like "I think you're finally getting it" will be interpreted as phony and insulting. Treat each student respectfully, and accept the fact that some kids will need a lot more teaching than others.

Another behavior that must be avoided at all times is cursing. This is more likely to happen, intentionally or unintentionally, during the stressful and frustrating times when kids lose self-control. Throughout these intense situations, monitor your frustration level and be aware of what you are saying. Cursing or swearing is extremely unprofessional and poor modeling, and it also is a sure-fire way of intensifying a child's inappropriate behavior and badly damaging relationships. Simply, if you lose control and start cursing at a student, that behavior will come back to haunt you. Students will think you condone cursing because you have modeled that behavior yourself.

Be careful not to use commands or statements like "You need to quit arguing" or "Sit down right now." These statements irritate kids and further escalate their behaviors. As the student becomes more and more upset, you may start to lose your temper.

Considering your word choice when making a request of a student allows you to remain calm and helps to keep the youngster's negative behavior from escalating. Try requests such as "Would you please stop talking?" or "A better choice would be to sit down." These send the same message as a command, but in a more gentle way. Making requests in this type of calm, cool, and collected manner increases the chances that a student will comply and successfully work through a crisis.

▶ **Use statements of empathy, understanding, and concern.** It is extremely hard for anyone – including adults – to calm down when they are angry or frustrated. Expecting kids to calm down quickly is unrealistic.

Showing empathy and concern for an upset youth helps defuse the highly charged emotions that can erupt during a crisis. Statements like "I know it's really hard to pull yourself together when you're upset" or "You are really upset, and I want to help you work through this so you can feel better" let students know that you understand what they are experiencing and are concerned about their well-being. Statements of concern and understanding are extremely effective in helping you and the student calm down.

Remember that empathy statements work best with students with whom you have a strong relationship. This doesn't mean that you shouldn't use empathy with a youth you don't know well, but make certain the words you use sound genuine, because a phony-sounding comment will only make matters worse between you and the student.

When you hear responses from kids such as "You don't know how I feel!" or "You don't really care about me!", it means you are grating on their nerves and should stop using these statements. However, this may be an opportunity to use a concern statement like "I can see that you're really upset."

Generally, it may be more effective to use empathy when a student is depressed, sad, or lonely, than when he or she is angry or aggressive.

▶ **Use positive correction.** At some time during your teaching career, you will give a negative consequence for a student's negative behavior. This may involve something like imposing a detention or the student losing time on the classroom computer.

Many times when this happens, kids don't see any light at the end of the tunnel and they focus solely on what they just lost. That is why it's important to tell students they will have a chance to earn back some of the consequence by practicing behavior that you want to see. We call this ray of hope a positive correction statement.

It may be just what the student needs to hear to calm down. An example might be: "Casey, remember that you will have a chance to earn some of your computer time back when you calm down and start working."

Use positive correction selectively. A good rule of thumb is not to let a youth earn back more than half of the consequence. So, if a student earned an hour after-school detention, then the most he or she could earn back would be a half-hour. How much a student earns back depends on how serious the behavior was and how long it took the student to regain control and begin taking direction from you.

▶ **Know your student.** Every student has unique needs, and the way you teach will vary accordingly. You'll have to take many variables into consideration when deciding what techniques to use.

One of the most important variables is your relationship with the student. When you have a positive relationship, the student is more likely to listen to you, want to please you, and follow instructions. In this situation, you'll be able to use humor, nicknames, or shared experiences – in carefully selected teaching settings – as a way to reach out to the student. These same qualities, when used by a caregiver who does not have a strong relationship with a youth, may be perceived as sarcastic, condescending, or meaningless.

Another factor to keep in mind when trying to forge relationships with students is to wipe the slate clean after a crisis. Even though a youth may have used hurtful words, you must treat what the youth said as behaviors and not as personal attacks. This isn't easy to do, but it is effective in building a relationship. A young person needs to know that their past negative behavior will not be dredged up as a constant reminder that he or she made a bad choice. Kids need support in crisis situations, not a verbal replay of the mistakes they've made.

Other important variables are a student's age and developmental level. With an older youth, you may be able to use logic to defuse a crisis situation. Some older students respond to teaching that explains the effect their behavior has on others. With younger students, you may have to be firmer, use simpler words, and make the teaching process shorter to capture their shorter attention span.

Teaching kids skills and self-control techniques is an interactive process. If you aren't careful, some kids may try and manipulate you and "teach" you to use inappropriate behaviors. It is important to know what behaviors trigger negative thoughts and behaviors in you, so you can be aware when you're becoming upset.

Unless you are in control of yourself, it is impossible to teach a student how to maintain self-control. When you remain calm, the stu-

dents have the time they need to calm down and think about the self-control strategies they want to use. The goal is not to control children, but to teach them how to exercise self-control.

Chapter Summary

Crisis Teaching: A teaching process that helps students regain self-control and make good decisions in times of conflict, and teaches skills that help students manage their response the next time.

Step-by-Step

    Address the problem behavior

    Monitor your self-control

    Ensure student self-control

    Engage student in follow-up teaching or problem-solving

Benefits of Crisis Teaching

    A reliable, structured teaching system to use in a crisis situation

    Techniques for teaching the student self-control

Using Crisis Teaching

    Remain calm, patient

    Keep aware of physical actions

    Know when to teach and when to listen

Relationship Components of Crisis Teaching

    Offer the student cool-down time

    Focus on what the student is doing right

    Talk softly, slowly

    Remain relaxed

    Avoid arguing

    Watch your words

    Use empathy statements

    Use positive correction

    Know your student

Making a
Difference

ChapterSeven

Forging Relationships with Students

It's Tuesday morning in a large high school in a big city, and students are moving from one class to the next. The hallways are noisy, filled with boisterous teenagers, who yell and jostle each other as they move through the crowded passageways.

Mavis Duncan sits at her desk in her classroom, chatting with John Drew. Both are math teachers at the school. With them is Toni Walker, a visiting teacher from a nearby rural district. Miss Walker is spending the day observing a new curriculum that Mrs. Duncan and Mr. Drew have developed.

As the three sit in the classroom, a student in the hallway yells "F--- you!" and suddenly a slight teenage boy with long blond hair hurtles into the classroom laughing. He struggles to keep his balance, having been shoved through the open doorway by the screaming student in the hallway. Then, the intruder yells back, "You a------," and makes a beeline for the door, disappearing almost as quickly as he has appeared.

Mrs. Duncan and Mr. Drew continue chatting, oblivious to the commotion around them.

Miss Walker looks at the other two teachers. "Why didn't you say something to that kid?" she asks.

Mrs. Duncan looks bewildered, then shrugs. "I don't know him," she says.

Jesus Perez is sitting in his counselor's office, where he's been summoned to discuss his plummeting grades in World Geography.

"I'm trying to understand why you're on the verge of a D, when you're doing so well in your other classes," counselor Jim Armstrong tells Perez.

The boy remains quiet, staring straight ahead. Finally, he says, "My name is Jesus – 'HAY-ZOOS.' That teacher's been calling me 'GEE-ZUZ' since the first day. He didn't even try to get my name right. Why should I try?"

◆ Getting to Know Students

Sometimes, we put up walls between ourselves and our students. In some cases, as in the first example, the walls may go up because we feel the need to filter out some of the noise and confusion that's part of working in a busy school. We know that we can't help every student in school, so we pull back, sometimes keeping our efforts to a bare minimum.

Unfortunately, minimum effort won't cut it these days. We have to take control by whatever safe and effective means we can in order to redeem our school buildings from the violence that's overwhelming them. Even small actions can make a difference. Consider the teacher we heard about who kept waiting for the custodians to come to her classroom and remove the "F--- Off!" graffiti scrawled in permanent marker on her bulletin board. Those powerful, angry words screamed out every day for a week to the students sitting in her classroom.

By not covering the epithet with a poster or filling in the "F" and "u" to make the message say "Back Off!", the teacher was giving the written outburst power over her classroom. By not taking some action herself against the graffiti, she was letting it disrupt her teaching space, showing her students that it was somehow okay to be there.

In the example with Jesus, the teacher didn't purposely mispronounce the student's name. But by failing to learn the correct pronunciation, he alienated the student from the first day, sabotaging any possibility of developing a relationship that could expand the student's chances for learning.

If the teacher had simply asked Jesus and other students how to pronounce their names on the first day of school, he'd have gotten the right pronunciation. Then he could have written the student's name phonetically in his grade book, to jog his memory until he learned how to pronounce it. And he wouldn't have damaged his relationship with the student.

You can connect with students by learning what they like to be called – avoiding, of course, nicknames that may inspire negative behaviors or images. It can take some time to learn names, particularly in large, culturally diverse schools, but getting someone's name correct is the most basic form of showing him or her your respect.

To help you remember details about students, you may want to jot down notes about your students' likes and dislikes, or information about their families – whatever helps you know more about them to make a meaningful connection.

Creating Relationships

Tearing down walls like these can help keep our schools safe. Taking the time to know your students and showing them that you care about them – in other words, building relationships with them – is every bit as important as teaching them history or mathematics.

Indeed, a positive relationship can be a foundation for increased learning. If a student knows you care about him as a person, he just might feel more like learning from you. And if a student cares about learning, he is less likely to spend time in your class acting out.

In developing relationships with students, your goal is not to become their best friend or counselor, but to establish a trusting, mutually respectful environment. That may be extremely difficult with some teenagers, especially those who constantly challenge you or those with whom your best hope is to get through the day without conflict.

As the two earlier stories show, forging relationships with students can start with simple acts, such as monitoring behavior, letting them know your expectations, or learning to pronounce their names as a first step in learning about them.

But those relationships shouldn't end at the door of the classroom. Think of your entire school building – including hallways and the lunchroom – as a place for relationships with students to bloom and for learning to take root. When you do that, you not only expand opportunities to learn, but also make your buildings safer.

Teaching Beyond the Classroom

Research study after research study has shown that hallways, playgrounds, and cafeterias are the most likely areas for students to engage in disruptive and violent behaviors. That's because the student-teacher ratio increases to about 200 to 1 in these areas, there is little structure, and frequently there is not enough adult supervision.

Teachers realize this is a problem, but many don't see hallways, playgrounds, and cafeterias as part of their teaching venue, unless they have supervision duty in one of those areas that day. Many believe their professional responsibilities lie only in the classroom, or they fear getting hurt by angry, out-of-control students (Astor, 1998).

Those are understandable concerns, but they must be balanced against the violence buffeting our schools these days. If teachers begin viewing the entire school building – rather than just the classroom – as a place where learning can occur, violent activities in schools may be reduced. This new vision requires extra effort, yes, but ultimately that effort may pay off in better behavior from students and less overall

chaos. If students know they are being watched as they move throughout the school building, there's a good chance their negative behaviors will decline.

Try this for a week: Stand outside your classroom between classes and greet students as they pass by in the hallway or move into your room. Keep an eye on what's happening in the hall. If somebody's too rowdy, remind him or her to take it easy. If you see a student who just needs an encouraging smile, give him one.

Besides making themselves more visible during passing periods and in volatile settings like the cafeteria, teachers also can regularly remind students of the procedure the school has in place for any less-structured setting. For more information on how to initiate these types of discussions with students, see Chapter 9 on Proactive Teaching.

Another way to increase supervision of students is for teachers to work more closely with other members of the school staff such as school police officers or interventionists. Working as a team, educators and other staff members can identify potential problems – both human and situational – and find ways to defuse them before they grow out of proportion.

But where do we start? In large schools with burgeoning enrollments, the task may seem overwhelming, but it really boils down to each teacher reaching out to one student – making a difference, one student at a time.

◆ Tuning In and Reaching Out

Cathy could hardly believe it when her 13-year-old son Eric came home from junior high one day and told her about his buddy, Tommy.

"Tommy's rich, Mom," Eric said.

"What do you mean? Did his parents win the lottery?"

"No, Mom, but he brought $3,000 to school. It was all in hundred-dollar bills."

"What?" Cathy said, unbelieving. "Where did he get that kind of money?"

"It's his dad's. He sold a baseball card and got paid in cash. Tommy was showing it off to other kids like it was his, but he told me it was really his dad's."

"What did your teachers say about him having that money?"

"Well, nobody said anything, but I know Miss Moore knew about the money, because we told her. I guess she just wasn't paying attention."

If ever there was a time for teachers to pay attention to what is going on in their schools, this is it. If teachers and school staff don't question a junior high student about bringing $3,000 to school, how easy is it going to be to bring a weapon into the building?

Tune in to students – not just the ones in your classes, but all students in the building. Listen to their conversations. Watch what they do. Be aware of items they bring to school and what they're discussing with their friends. Know what popular slang terms mean. Your observations may stop a problem before it escalates.

By working to establish solid relationships with kids and developing a schoolwide monitoring and intervention system, we can restore our buildings to the places of learning they once were and begin to uproot violence. We can take back our schools.

A big part of that effort is building positive relationships with students, particularly those who have aggressive or violent tendencies. Many of these youngsters have had trouble making and keeping friends, and they probably have had little success developing relationships with adults in authority, such as parents, teachers, and employers. Yet, developing these positive relationships is a key to living a rewarding and happy life.

Following nearly all the fatal school shootings in this country, shockingly similar profiles of the youth involved have emerged. Most are characterized as isolated youngsters who made threats or displayed other behaviors that were clearly cries for help. But no one took them seriously. No one bothered to listen.

Think about your school. There are young people you see every day who could benefit from the support of a caring teacher. If you are able to nurture relationships with these students, you are more likely to become a valuable role model for them, laying the foundation for teaching essential lessons. In addition, the relationship should enhance students' self-confidence, and that could lead to improvements in behavior. The more students value the relationship, the more likely they are to continue behaving appropriately and the more open they will be to learning.

◆ Tolerances and Teaching Procedures

Two concepts that are important for helping students learn to develop relationships are tolerance level and teaching procedures.

Tolerance level refers to the expectations you have about what student behaviors you will accept and those you will not accept. These might include your expectations for how class assignments are to be completed and expectations for how students respond during class discussions or question-and-answer periods. You also have expectations for how students will treat you in the classroom and how they will treat each other.

In a classroom with a high tolerance level, a great deal of inappropriate behavior will be allowed. In a classroom with a low tolerance level, clearly understood rules will govern behavior and very little inappropriate behavior will be permitted.

A classroom with a high tolerance level might be a fun place for students, and they might think you're a cool teacher, but there's a good chance they won't be learning much because of the lack of structure.

However, a classroom with too much structure, characterized by extremely low tolerances, lack of warmth, and lots of rules, might make a lousy place to learn, too. That's because such a regimented setting isn't conducive to student-teacher relationships or cooperative learning between peers.

Try taking a middle road between these two extremes. Remember that you can have low tolerances *and* still build positive relationships. In fact, our research shows that kids appreciate the structure and safety low tolerances provide when teachers develop those tolerances in a positive and caring manner.

Don't think your students will consider you cool if you cut them some behavioral slack or let them get by with inappropriate behaviors. Raising tolerance levels will not help build relationships and will not help youths learn the skills they need to be able to develop relationships.

Low tolerances are important if youngsters are to learn the skills they need in order to develop relationships. High tolerances send a message to students that inappropriate behavior is acceptable. Accepting problem behaviors inadvertently reinforces and strengthens the behavior. Therefore, you'll see more of that bad behavior.

When tolerances are too high, youth are confused about what is and what is not acceptable. Students also are "set up" for failure in other settings, since other adults in authority are unlikely to tolerate such problem behavior. In effect, you place students at greater risk when your tolerance levels are high.

In addition to maintaining low tolerances, teachers also must strive for consistency in their contacts with students. Maintaining consistency in what you will accept as appropriate behavior reduces student confusion, helps them understand expectations, and makes it easier for them to learn and maintain skills. Consistency also reduces conflict between you and your students.

Take time to examine your own behavior with students. Do you find yourself spending more time correcting a student than offering praise? Then make a conscious effort to add positive comments and praise to your dialogue with that student. Sometimes it's difficult to come to the end of a long, tiring day and force yourself to analyze your relationship with a student, but it may be the only way to track the progress you are making. Ask yourself what you have done well with the student and what efforts need more work.

The time you spend teaching youngsters academic and social skills also builds relationships. Effective Praise and Proactive Teaching, with their focus on positive reinforcement, are particularly good tools for establishing relationships. Both Effective Praise and Proactive Teaching are explained in detail later in this book.

Also keep the following classroom- and academic-based considerations in mind as you work to define and improve relationships with your students:

▶ **Class Atmosphere:** *On the day following the massacre at Columbine High School in Littleton, Colo., a student in a Midwestern classroom raised his hand and posed a question: "When is somebody going to talk to us about Littleton? I think we need to talk about it."*

"Science is what we're talking about," the boy's teacher replied curtly.

The Columbine shootings broke the heart of a quiet Colorado community and stunned a nation. It's horrific to think that 12 students and a teacher could be gunned down by two classmates in a suburban high school, but it happened.

How would you have answered the student who wanted to talk about the shooting? Is your classroom atmosphere open to a discussion of such a difficult topic?

The tone you set in your classroom is crucial not only for teaching students science or math or English, but also for teaching them essential life lessons – getting along with others and making some sense out of the world.

Take a look at your classroom atmosphere. Have you established a setting where students feel free to ask questions, where they know they can have a meaningful dialogue, where they do not feel persecuted?

Does the atmosphere in your classroom communicate respect? Do you refuse to tolerate bullies and those who would ridicule another student's differences? Do you consistently enforce rules?

Think about your answers to these questions. Then think about the powerful lesson that the science teacher taught her students when she refused to discuss Columbine – that their safety isn't part of her curriculum.

Had she taken the time to talk about the Colorado massacre, the teacher might have had an opportunity to engage in a real dialogue with students about the fear and the anger they feel because of what happened at Littleton. And the teacher might have had a chance to talk about the very real issue of alienation, perhaps opening a door to a student who felt isolated and desperately alone.

▶ **Physical Environment:** Does your classroom's physical layout reflect your commitment to learning? Is your classroom decorated attractively? Is the room free of litter and clutter and maintained regularly? Is your classroom arranged in a way that's conducive to including and monitoring all students?

▶ **Instructional Style and Techniques:** Do you vary your teaching style and techniques to accommodate the changing needs of students and the material you are presenting? Variety may keep both you and your students interested in the process.

▶ **Instructional Efficiency:** Are your lesson plans and classroom activities well organized? Do lesson plans have purpose and measurable outcomes? Do lessons begin and end on time? Does instructional pace promote attentiveness? Is transition time minimal? Do you take cultural diversity into account when you plan lessons?

▶ **Monitoring Student Progress:** Do you check for student understanding as you teach and make adjustments to ensure lessons are having an impact on students? Do you praise students, offer encouragement, and prompt students in what's appropriate? Do you keep data on student performance and maintain records?

The following qualities also help build relationships:

▶ **Listening:** The skill of listening cannot be overemphasized. Much of our communication with other people is accomplished without saying a word. Listening demonstrates caring, interest, and warmth.

Young people need to have someone listen to what they have to say. Many kids have not yet learned how to express themselves. At times, they feel one way, but their words say something else. By listening carefully, you can pick up on cues that indicate what is troubling a student. Sometimes, you may have to restate or rephrase what the youth said. You can ask questions that may help a young person find a solution to a problem. You can label feelings and emotions and explain how they affect behavior.

Sometimes, kids say "off-the-wall" things just to get our attention or indicate that something is bothering them. A simple "Would you like to talk about it?" can open the door to a meaningful interaction. A great deal of teaching can be done if you are attentive and really listen.

▶ **Tone of Voice:** Make sure your voice tone matches the message you are trying to give. This means being aware of how loud or soft and how slow or fast your conversation is. Often, young people will remember the way you said something longer and better than the actual words you said. For example, speaking softly and slowly may help soothe an angry student. An enthusiastic voice may encourage him or her to try harder. A sarcastic voice shows that you aren't sincere, regardless of what you say.

▶ **Touch:** Physical touch is a powerful communicator. It shows warmth and acceptance. A pat on the back or an arm around the shoulder can comfort a sad or lonely teenager. Shaking hands or "giving five" can show your approval and satisfaction.

Of course, touch can be misused and misunderstood. Touch should never be threatening, intimidating, or sexual in nature. It is crucial that you give kids their "personal space" because it shows you respect their right to privacy.

▶ **Eye Contact and Body Language:** Looking at the student is very important. If you never look up from your book or papers, a young person will think you don't care. You also will miss an opportunity to watch the student's facial expressions, which can help you determine what he or she is feeling. Use facial expressions and body language that show you are interested. Smile, nod your head, and keep your arms and hands relaxed. Face the student, and stand or sit close by while still giving him or her some personal space. Your eye contact, facial expressions, and posture indicate your willingness to listen.

▶ **Understanding:** Kids live in their "kid world," just as we live in our "adult world." Those worlds don't always exist in perfect harmony. Often, when kids try to explain a dilemma in their lives, adults say something like, "That's not a problem. Wait until you're older, then you'll know what real problems are." That's the same as saying, "Go away, kid. You're bothering me."

Try to see things from the youth's perspective. If a young person feels like sharing something with you, listen attentively. In fact, you should feel good that he or she trusted you enough to ask for your help. All ages and developmental stages bring new problems into a young person's life. Be understanding and listen carefully. What may seem like a minor problem to you could be monumental to a young person.

Do you remember your teen-age years? Remember the roller coaster of emotions? One day you're on top of the world, and the next day you wonder if life is worth living. Keep that roller coaster image in mind as you work with your students, and remember that frequent affirmation is a great leveler for them. Just taking time to listen to a student is very affirming.

▶ **Play:** There's a little kid in each of us, but some adults won't let that little kid out to play. Playing is serious stuff; it teaches valuable lessons about life, including sharing, respecting others, taking responsibility, and following the rules.

You can incorporate elements of play into your classroom. One teacher we worked with divided her classroom into teams and had students come up with questions to ask each other on a subject they were studying. After the students handed in the questions, the teacher assigned point values to each question, based on its difficulty. Then, each Friday, the teacher had a contest where students answered the questions to earn points. Occasionally, she even videotaped the contest. It was a novel and exciting way to teach the class material, have fun, and help students develop relationships with each other.

▶ **Humor:** Having a good sense of humor can be an invaluable tool in the classroom. Humor is an excellent way to forge relationships with students, to show them that you're human and approachable. It's also a good way to model behavior for your students. Kids need to learn how to find humor in life and to realize how healthy it is to laugh. Kids need a break from their stresses just as much as adults do.

Dealing with kids is a tough business that's full of ups and downs. If you don't learn how to find humor in what happens, you will constantly dwell on all the bad things. A good sense of humor can insulate you from negative feelings that can get the best of you.

You don't have to be a stand-up comedian to use humor in your classroom. The point is to communicate to your students that you have a sense of humor and to create a pleasant classroom environment. Choose a method that suits your personality. It might be something as simple as cutting out comic strips that pertain to something your class is studying or something that's going on in your school.

Or maybe you're a good storyteller and can use funny stories to convey some of the lessons you teach. Perhaps your sense of humor leans more toward the use of exaggeration and understatement, and you can bring a smile to students' faces with remarks like "He must have eaten a bazillion tacos" or "I'm so broke, I can't even pay attention."

Whatever method you use, it's important to make your humor a natural extension of your personality. Used in this way, humor provides welcome relief from the everyday stresses of life, and allows us to relax and enjoy each other.

Also, don't be afraid to let your students express their senses of humor in your class. We're not talking about grooming a roomful of class clowns, just letting jokes and gentle teasing have a place alongside academics and making your classroom a fun, comfortable place to learn.

For example, one teacher had a student named Kevin who was much smaller than the other students in the chemistry class. One day, one of the other boys was trying to open up a chemical bottle to do an experiment, but he couldn't get the bottle cap to budge. Kevin tried and unscrewed the top the first time! From then on, Kevin was good-naturedly called "Hulk" by the rest of the class.

Every time someone called him by his nickname, he'd laugh, flex his muscles, and let out a grunt like a weight-lifter. The teasing was done in a tasteful and caring way. Kevin knew the others weren't making fun of him, and the attention made him feel special.

▶ **Empathy:** Empathy means trying to understand another person's situation and feelings. For many people, this is not easy or natural. Many of us grew up being told what we should do and how we should feel. In fact, many of us may even have been taught to deny our true feelings. We heard statements like "You really don't mean that" or "There's no reason to feel that way. Straighten up and fly right."

Although these statements may be appropriate occasionally, they don't have much effect on changing a teen's behavior. And often, the harder you try to convince students that they really aren't feeling what they say they're feeling, the more those feelings seem to stick with them.

Kids go through many changes, and often they don't know how to handle new experiences and the emotions that these changes bring. Sometimes, they may feel trapped by their feelings and think that any attempt to change is futile.

You can steer students through the minefield of emotions by validating their feelings, by assuring them that their confusion or sadness or anger is perfectly okay. But how they act on those feelings can have an impact – positive or negative – on themselves or others.

A kind and caring adult can help a youngster begin the process of hope and healing. Kids need to learn that negative emotions are a transient part of life and that things will get better. You can teach them that it's okay to feel bad; more importantly, you can help them find the strength in themselves to carry on.

We all know that it's easy to talk to a young person when he or she is happy and has a posi-

tive outlook. Dealing constructively with a youth's negative feelings requires much more skill. Using empathy involves identifying with what a person is going through. One thing that helps is to think back to the way that you felt in similar situations. Empathy requires you to look at the world through your student's eyes.

Many young people, especially those who use aggressive and violent behaviors, also face the problem of not having a trusted adult in whom they can confide. Their negative behaviors have alienated many people. In addition, youngsters these days face more pressure and experience it sooner than prior generations. Many are forced to grow up too fast.

Furthermore, a larger proportion of youth than ever before come from dysfunctional or abusive backgrounds, where they may be deprived of the love and discipline they need. They may need someone with whom they can share their fear and pain, but they may not know how to ask for help. You may have to look for signs – subtle and otherwise – that they're ready to share their feelings.

Once you have established a solid relationship with a student, you'll be able to talk frankly with him or her about the importance of asking for help when needed. Many times, teenagers are embarrassed to seek help, especially if the problem is a personal one. You can let them know that you and others who care about them always are available, and that it's better to seek advice from an objective person than to take an action that might hurt someone or make the situation worse.

Remember that empathy does not replace teaching and consequences. Students need to learn that feeling bad is not an excuse for misbehavior. Just because you're angry at your boss doesn't mean you can punch him in the nose. As a teacher, you may have empathy for a student who's going through a difficult time, but that doesn't mean you should protect students from the consequences of their inappropriate behavior.

To use empathy effectively, mean what you say. Use a soft, comforting voice, and watch the student's reaction. Offer to help, if necessary, and follow up. If you know one of your students was feeling depressed, check later to see if he or she is doing better. Remember how you felt in similar situations, what you did to escape those emotional ruts, and how other people helped you.

Some adults rush to solve a youth's problem. They feel that having all of the answers is their primary role. But, while giving advice and instructions is very important, there are times when it's best just to listen and understand. Be patient; there will be time to solve the problems later.

Always rushing to offer a solution can be a real turn-off for the student. There are times in life when each of us merely wants to feel that someone is on our side. As you build relationships with your students, you will learn to gauge when and when not to offer solutions or empathy. Later in this book, we'll discuss methods for helping students learn to take responsibility for their own problems and develop problem-solving skills.

▶ **Praise:** Praise is nourishment. It helps students grow emotionally, just as food helps them grow physically. In the classroom, praise is a vital learning tool. Read Chapter 8 on Effective Praise in this book for information on using this particular teaching tool. Below are some other aspects of praise to keep in mind.

▶ **Be specific at first:** Praise behavior in a way that the youth understands so he or she has enough information to fully understand how or why to continue the good behavior. Later, you will move from specific to generalized praise. When you first start working with a young person, say things such as "Jamie, thanks for being on time this morning. We can get started now without any delay." In this way, students will know what behaviors you approve of and want to see again.

▶ **Give generalized praise:** As your students internalize positive behaviors, you can gradually move to more generalized praise because too much specific praise can be non-reinforcing or irritating, and can even appear condescending. Sometimes, a simple statement like "Good job" is enough to make the youth feel valued for his or her special qualities. Kids progress at different rates, and your praise should be adjusted according to their age and ability to understand. Also, you can show appreciation by pointing out a student's overall qualities with comments such as "You really stick with a task until it's done." Respect the uniqueness of your kids and recognize what makes each of them feel worthwhile and accepted.

▶ **Be brief and enthusiastic:** Too much praise sounds phony. Keep your comments simple and age-appropriate. And deliver the praise with real emotion in your voice. Show your students how good you feel about them meeting expectations.

▶ **Give praise at appropriate times:** Usually, it's best to give praise immediately, but there may be situations when it's better to wait. For example, some of your students won't like to be praised in front of others; it embarrasses them. Some kids like a "thumbs up" or a simple head nod showing approval better than words. Some kids like loud, boisterous cheerleading-like praise. Others like a softer, more sensitive style. Find out what works for each youth in order to make the praise meaningful.

Chapter Summary

Forging Relationships with Students

Getting to Know Students
Creating relationships
Teaching beyond the classroom

Tuning In and Reaching Out

Tolerances and Teaching Procedures
Class atmosphere
Physical environment
Instructional style/techniques
Instructional efficiency
Monitoring student progress
Listening
Tone of voice
Touch
Eye contact and body language
Understanding
Play
Humor
Empathy
Praise

ChapterEight

Effective Praise

Jermaine is a student who has trouble accepting criticism. Whenever his teacher, Grant Brooks, asks Jermaine to make corrections in his homework, Jermaine rolls his eyes, starts an argument with the teacher, and frequently says something whiny, like "Why are you making me do this?"

Last Tuesday, Mr. Brooks returned a paper to Jermaine and asked the student to correct several sentences where the subject and verb did not agree. Jermaine gave a heavy sigh but did not argue. "Okay," he said. "I'll take care of it."

The lack of argument was not lost on Mr. Brooks, and he immediately began to praise Jermaine. "Jermaine, I really appreciate you not arguing with me. When you accept criticism like that, you show me you're taking responsibility. That will show people they can work with you. Do you see what I mean?"

"Yes, Mr. Brooks."

"Great! You know what? Since you didn't argue, it looks like you'll have some extra time

to finish those corrections in class, so you won't have homework tonight. Good job, Jermaine."

Praise is a powerful tool for changing, improving, and maintaining the behaviors of your students. It is crucial to the development of positive relationships between you and your students and is very important to strengthen appropriate behavior. **Effective Praise** is a teaching process that combines praise, reasons, and positive consequences to reinforce a specific behavior. It allows you to individualize your teaching of social skills by enthusiastically and sincerely recognizing each student's efforts and progress.

Effective Praise is specific, genuine, and contingent on appropriate behavior. It should be totally positive because you recognize appropriate behavior and pair specific descriptions with positive consequences.

This means you should look carefully for opportunities to praise and reinforce a student's efforts toward positive behavior. There's a saying we have here at Boys Town that describes this process. We call it "catch 'em being good." Seizing the chance to praise appropriate behavior increases the odds that the desired behavior will occur again.

Effective Praise is used in connection with two other kinds of praise, general and specific praise. General praise is a broad statement such as "You did a nice job." Specific praise pinpoints certain behavior such as "You did a nice job on the fifth problem."

When you begin to work with students, you will start with Effective Praise, which will help you shape skills that are not firmly in students' repertoires by giving youngsters significant feedback. As you begin to develop relationships with students and their skills develop, you will be able to pare back the amount of praise you use, moving from Effective to specific to general.

Keep in mind that your praise must not sound phony and must be contingent on behavior, especially when you're working with older students. Coupling praise with an empathy statement is a powerful tool you can use with older students. For example, you could say to a chronically tardy student, "Gosh, Kevin, it must have been tough getting yourself here on time today with this snow. Good job!"

◆ Effective Praise: A Step-by-Step Look

Here's a look at the four steps of Effective Praise:

1. Describe the appropriate behavior.
2. Give a rationale.
3. Request acknowledgement.
4. Give a positive consequence.

▶ **Describe the appropriate behavior:** Use specific words to tell the student what he or she has just done right, and break the action into steps, then label the skill you're talking about. **Example:** "Amy, I know disagreeing appropriately with an adult is tough. You did a nice job of staying calm and telling me exactly what you thought I graded incorrectly on your paper and why." Labeling skills and providing specific behavioral descriptions increase the odds that students will learn new ways to behave and can generalize the skills to future situations.

▶ **Give a rationale:** If you give students a reason for changing their behavior, they are more likely to adopt the new behavior. And teachers who provide rationales are viewed by students as more considerate and fair; rationales help build relationships with students. **Example:** "When you can disagree and stay cool at the same time, people are more likely to listen and they may be more willing to compromise."

▶ **Request acknowledgment:** Check to make sure the student is paying attention and understands your rationale by asking for acknowledgment. Although this is a specific step in the sequence, requests for acknowledgment should take place throughout any teaching. **Example:** "Do you understand?" or "Does that make sense?" Requesting acknowledgment creates a dialogue with the student so the teaching process doesn't seem like a lecture.

▶ **Give a positive consequence:** Positive consequences help promote constructive, rapid behavior change when paired with specific skill teaching. Tell the student what positive consequence he or she has earned for engaging in the specific appropriate behavior. **Example:** "I'll tell you what: I'll look at your paper again. I may not change my mind about the correction, but for talking to me about your concerns and advocating for yourself and your work, you've earned five extra credit points." In order for positive consequences to reinforce behavior, they must meet several conditions. Positive consequences must be individualized, depending on the child's interests. Also, make sure the size of the reinforcer is appropriate, just large enough to maintain or increase the behavior. Remember there are many kinds of reinforcers – tangibles (passes, food); activities (time to visit with classmates, working on the computer), and social ("Good job!", a pat on the back). Use the reinforcer that has demonstrated a positive effect on the student's behavior in the past.

◆ Effective Praise Variations

In a busy classroom, you probably have little spare time, and the typical four steps of Effective Praise may seem like they take too much time. You don't always have to use all the steps to be effective. Some variations are shown below.

▶ **General Praise/Label Skill & Consequence:** "Nice job of following instructions on the test, Jodie. You've earned an extra 10 minutes of computer time this afternoon."

▶ **General Praise/Label Skill & Rationale:** "Thanks for accepting my decision. When you take supervision like that, you show leadership."

◆ Benefits of Effective Praise

Effective Praise helps develop positive relationships between you and your students. Many students, particularly those with aggressive tendencies, have difficulty developing constructive relationships with adults in authority or in making or keeping friends. Effective Praise contributes substantially to helping each child learn and grow because you are recognizing the incremental gains being made by each student.

When you start using Effective Praise in your classroom, you may see some students begin engaging in "good" behavior to gain your attention and approval. You must guard against developing students who are merely obedient or compliant or are just performing.

Instead, you must work toward developing a sense of responsibility in students. By helping them realize the benefits they will receive, students will begin to develop an internalized set of values and motivation that will result in a sense of personal power (Miller, 1984). That should allow them to discard some of the aggressive behaviors they have been using.

Effective Praise increases learning and students' behavioral options. As you focus on what a student is doing well, you become more aware of the student's positive behaviors, creating a positive cycle of interactions. The more you're aware of what the student does "right," the more opportunities you have to address and increase positive behavior change. By reinforcing skills that fit societal norms, students increase their repertoire of behavioral responses and begin choosing behaviors that are more readily accepted by others.

◆ How to Use Effective Praise

Effective Praise should be used only after a desired behavior occurs, not as a general motivator. By providing praise after a student has demonstrated a particular behavior, you link success with the student's effort. This tells the student that similar success can be attained again. It also helps students see that they are in charge of their own behavior.

Effective Praise should always specifically describe which behaviors are being recognized and reinforced. Use simple, direct statements to help the student understand what is being praised and lend credibility to your comments.

◆ When to Use Effective Praise

Use Effective Praise frequently to reinforce new skills. When students are learning something new, they need reinforcement every time they use the skill correctly. Continuous reinforcement builds and strengthens skills. For maximum effectiveness, try to use Effective Praise as quickly as you can after you spot a behavior you're trying to reinforce.

Effective Praise also is used when you are attempting to strengthen existing positive behaviors or build a skill's fluency. As a student demonstrates more frequent and appropriate use of a skill, you should use an intermittent schedule of reinforcement to maintain it. This "element of surprise" can reinforce the student's use of the skill. Using an intermittent schedule also helps with fading the use of reinforcers to a more realistic level.

When a student seems to have a behavior well-mastered, you can use general, nonspecific praise such as "Good job" or "Nice work on the project."

Most often, you will use Effective Praise privately, as public praise can be embarrassing and have counterproductive results. The one-on-one teaching provides complete and personal attention.

As you use Effective Praise with your students, pay close attention to *how* you are communicating. Look at the student. Use a pleasant voice. Say the student's name. Smile. Use appropriate humor and show enthusiasm.

Quality components such as these establish and maintain a productive climate for learning, as well as improve the relationships between you and your students.

Effective Praise and other positive teaching experiences with students should occur at least four times as often as you correct students. This 4:1 ratio enhances relationships, results in more positive behavior from your students, and helps build "reinforcement reserves" for students. The 4:1 ratio is a minimum standard; many children need higher ratios of positive-to-corrective feedback to show improvement.

Chapter Summary

Effective Praise: A teaching process that combines praise, reasons, and positive consequences to reinforce a specific behavior.

General praise: "You did a nice job."

Specific praise: "You did a nice job on the fifth problem."

A Step-by-Step Look

Describe the appropriate behavior

Give a rationale

Request acknowledgment

Give a positive consequence

Variations

Benefits of Effective Praise

Helps develop relationships between teachers and students

Increases sense of responsibility in students

Increases student learning and behavioral options

Using Effective Praise

After desired behavior occurs

Be specific

Use to reinforce newly acquired skills and to reinforce fluency

4:1 Ratio with corrections

ChapterNine

Proactive Teaching

On the first few days of Lauren Evans' high school Science Laboratory class each fall, she spends some time preparing her students for the year ahead.

"This class will be different from your other classes," Ms. Evans tells them. "We're going to do a lot of experiments, and that means not only working from our textbooks, but also working with each other and with lab equipment. So we need to go over some of the rules and procedures we will be following this year."

She reminds her students to bring their books to class every day because they will use them to do lab experiments and to complete worksheets.

And she spends time introducing students to the lab equipment they will use, including Bunsen burners, dissecting knives, and chemicals. She always devotes a lot of time to describing safety issues, explaining how hot the burners are and reviewing what to do if something spills or breaks. She even gives the students a quiz on the procedures to follow if there is a spill or breakage in the classroom, and she reminds them often to review the safety procedures chart on the back bulletin board. The chart lists the steps everyone is supposed to follow in an emergency, including a chemical spill, and what to do with broken glass beakers.

Finally, Ms. Evans talks to her students about their work groups. She leads a discussion on how people can successfully work together, getting students' suggestions on what cooperation means. She also organizes some fun team-building exercises to get the teenagers used to working together and following directions as a group.

Some of Ms. Evans' co-workers believe she spends too much time going over procedures, but she believes it is time well spent. She rarely has to spend time correcting students, and when the occasional spill or breakage occurs, her students handle the cleanup safely and efficiently. "My kids know what to expect in my classroom, *and because of that, they have more opportunities to learn," she says.*

◆ ◆ ◆

◆ Proactive Teaching

Teaching students life skills and academic skills is at the core of a Boys Town educational method called **Proactive Teaching.** Proactive Teaching is very simple, and it works. In fact, you've probably already used a form of Proactive Teaching with students in situations like fire drills or reviewing a syllabus at the beginning of a semester.

Proactive Teaching is a way to prevent problems by telling students what to do and having them practice before they encounter a specific situation.

Proactive Teaching is most effective when students are learning something new or when they have had difficulty in a past situation. Though it can be used in many areas, it is an especially good tool for helping youngsters learn positive ways to respond in situations where they have resorted to aggressive behaviors in the past.

As Ms. Evans showed in the earlier scenario, Proactive Teaching outlines the nuts and bolts of a situation that students are likely to encounter or the components of a skill they need to master.

When you teach proactively, you explore with students what will be expected of them in a certain setting. This "up front" teaching hopefully will help them face situations with more confidence and find success more frequently.

And when you apply Proactive Teaching concepts in your classroom, students learn what your expectations are, which improves how your classroom runs and increases learning time. It's best to use Proactive Teaching when students are calm and attentive, not after a misbehavior or when they are upset.

Following is an example of how Proactive Teaching might sound when the teacher and class are discussing an academic topic:

It's mid-September and Delores Lawrence is introducing the members of her Journalism I class to the concept of how to use quotes in a newspaper story.

"Let's start our discussion today with a definition. What is a quote? Kevin, can you answer that?"

"It's what somebody said," answers Kevin.

"That's right. And remember it's crucial to listen carefully to what the person is saying and to write down their words exactly. Reporters must get their facts straight. If their stories aren't accurate, no one will want to talk with them because they can't trust them to get things right. Do you see why it's important to be accurate?"

"Yeah," says Kelli. "If people won't talk to you, then there's no way you can do your stories."

"That's right, Kelli. Reporting is all about credibility. What are some things you can do to make sure that you're getting people's quotes accurately?"

"You could use a tape recorder," says one student.

"That's a good idea. A lot of reporters use tape recorders, and it's a good idea, but remember that you'll have to transcribe the tape before you write your story, so that will take more time. And even though you use a tape recorder, you still have to listen very carefully and you should still take good notes, okay?"

Students nod.

"Now let's talk about the kinds of quotes there are – direct quotes, partial quotes, and par-

aphrases." The teacher uses an overhead projector with examples to lead the class in a discussion about each type of quote. She asks a lot of questions to get students involved in the lesson, and she talks to them about the grammar rules involved in using quotes, including the use of quote marks.

"It's important to learn the style rules for quotes," Mrs. Lawrence tells the class, "Because then you can concentrate on your writing. And when I edit your stories, I'll know that you've learned the rules, and I can spend my time looking at what you have to say. Does that make sense?"

The students agree.

For a class activity, she stages a mock press conference about a plane crash in which a famous rock 'n' roll singer is killed.

The teacher tells the students that their assignment for the next class is to write a story about the plane crash based on information they get from the press conference. Their stories must have two direct quotes, two partial quotes, and two paraphrases. The teacher tape-records the press conference so she can check the students' quotes.

She gives her students basic information about the crash, then she takes the role of a spokesperson for the local sheriff's office, which is conducting the press conference. She instructs the students to raise their hands and ask her questions about the crash

During the next class, the students review their stories, and then compare what they wrote to newspaper accounts of the February 1959 plane crash in which rockers Buddy Holly, Ritchie Valens, and the Big Bopper were killed.

◆ ◆ ◆

As you can see, Proactive Teaching has many of the elements of "Direct Instruction," or "Stand and Deliver" teaching. You're introducing new concepts to students, so you're going to find out what knowledge base they may already have about a subject. You ask questions to see what they already know. Then you introduce new information to broaden their base. Finally, you expose students to a variety of opportunities to use their new knowledge, to maximize its potential for them. Let's look at Proactive Teaching in more detail.

There are two kinds of Proactive Teaching – Planned Teaching and the Preventive Prompt.

▶ **Planned Teaching** occurs when you teach a student a new skill or review a skill previously taught.

An example of Planned Teaching is an all-school assembly at the beginning of the year, when students learn about the consequences for being tardy or for being in hallways without permission during class time.

An example of Planned Teaching on an individual level might be helping a student develop a way to approach his boss and ask for time off to attend a student leadership conference.

▶ **Preventive Prompts** are simply brief reminders to students to behave in a way they have been taught. For example, if you have a student who is frequently late for your fourth-period class, you might prompt him by saying, "Steve, remember to be on time tomorrow, or you'll have your third tardy, and that's counted as an unexcused absence."

Or, you might say to your Algebra class: "You'll have 15 minutes for the quiz. Remember to show your work or the problem will be counted wrong."

Another example might be in the classroom, when a teacher alerts students to the end of the period by saying, "Two-minute warning!" The students know that's the time to put away their materials and get ready for the next class.

The Preventive Prompt is a powerful teaching tool because it is simple, easy to use, and can be applied in diverse situations. The following story shows how a Preventive Prompt might have come in handy in a classroom:

Joellen and LiAnne are chemistry partners. One day in class, when their teacher is out of the room, they accidentally break a glass beaker. It's a clean break, only two pieces, and the girls decide to try and glue it back together. They find some Superglue in the work area in the back of the classroom and carefully glue it back together, then pour a liquid chemical in it to see if it leaks.

Unfortunately, the chemical reacts with the Superglue, melting the beaker into a shapeless heap of glass. The chemical reaction leaves a big stain on the work counter. The girls have spent so much time on the beaker that they're now way behind the other students in the day's experiment. They decide to "'fess up" to their teacher, Oscar Contreras.

He is not happy about the mess but praises the girls for their honesty and attempt to solve the problem. Mr. Contreras realizes that he hasn't prompted his students about what to do if something breaks when he's not in the classroom.

During the next class period, the teacher spends a few minutes instructing the students to get Doris Schultz, the chemistry teacher next door, if he is not available. If something gets broken, he reminds them, they should get the dust pan and broom from the back corner of the classroom and sweep the broken glass into the paper sacks marked "Glass" that are stacked up

next to the wastebasket. They should report the accident to him.

Even if Mr. Contreras spends time during the first days of class talking to his students about what to do if an accident occurred, it's still a good idea to remind his class from time to time about the procedure to follow, just to keep the information fresh for them.

Proactive Teaching is a broad-based collection of strategies that you can use to help students find success both inside and outside the classroom. Many of the strategies also have the added benefit of ensuring student and school safety.

◆ Components of Proactive Teaching

Here's another example of Proactive Teaching:

Central High School has been plagued nearly every day recently by fights and skirmishes in the hallways and cafeteria. Teachers and staff are trying to figure out why there are so many fights. To get students' input on the problem, the principal has scheduled extended first periods on Tuesday morning and has asked teachers to lead discussions on the situation at that time. Sandra Tucker, a sophomore English teacher, starts the discussion in her classroom.

"Okay, everyone take your seats. We're going to talk about some of the problems that we've been having in the hallways and in the lunchroom. Some students I've talked to say the fights start because there are a lot of insults and accusations flying around out there. What do you think about that?"

A lot of murmuring fills the classroom. Many students nod their heads in agreement, and a couple of students raise their hands.

"Yes, Margie," Ms. Tucker says, acknowledging one student.

"Most times it's about somebody messin' with somebody's boyfriend or girlfriend," *the student suggests.*

"That makes sense," *the teacher says.* "What else gets fights started? Mickey?"

"Some people try to play games. They try to get into your head. Like they stare at you all the time, or they will be dissin' you."

Another student, Travis, pipes up: "They might say you're carrying some stuff just to see if they can get you in trouble, or they might say something about your sister."

"So let's talk about how some people react to accusations like this," *the teacher says.*

"Well, they'll just fight the other person right there," *says Adrian.*

"Or they'll say something bad back, and that will cause a fight," *Dara adds.*

"Good observations," *the teacher says.* "What usually happens if they fight or argue?"

"Then security comes and breaks it up, and the kids get sent to the office," *Travis answers.*

"Have you ever seen anybody get hurt when there's a fight?" *the teacher wonders.*

"Oh yeah," *says Travis.* "One of my partners, he got a black eye, and I saw a girl get cut from another girl's keys the other day."

"So let's think about other ways to respond to an insult. What are some things you could do that would make you feel in control but not earn you a consequence?"

"You could wait and fight the person after school," *Travis says with a twinkle in his eye, as the class laughs.*

"You know, that is an option, but it could lead to serious consequences and we're trying to find a solution that has fewer consequences, not more. So what other options would you have? Would you get real mad and clench your fists?"

"No," *several students say in chorus.*

"Right. You would try to stay calm. You wouldn't shout. You would use a quiet, even voice when you spoke. You could walk away. You might ask an adult to help you. Do you see a pattern here?"

The teacher pauses and scans the classroom. Eyes are on her, students are listening, so she continues.

"All these things are actions you can take; they are things you can do to control the outcome of the situation. You might think that you have to fight when somebody challenges you, but you don't have to. And if you don't fight, what happens?"

"People will call you a punk," *says a student from the back row, hoping for laughs. A few students chuckle.*

"You're right. Some people might call you that," *the teacher says.* "But they would be wrong, wouldn't they? And if you didn't fight, the very least that would happen would be that you won't get a detention and won't have to stay after school. And you know what? You also might feel pretty good about yourself, because you took some control and held on to it. Something else that might happen if you didn't fight could be that people see you in a different way. They see you as somebody who doesn't fight, instead of seeing you as somebody who gets in fights. That's a big difference, isn't it? If you have the reputation of somebody who fights, what's going to happen?"

"People will think you're going to fight a lot," *says Adrian.*

"Exactly, Adrian. They're going to expect you to fight or be in trouble, so if something bad happens, you are a prime suspect, because they already think you're a troublemaker. You get blamed, sometimes when you didn't even do anything, just 'cause the word out there about you is that you're trouble. Do you see what I'm saying?"

The students say "Yeah" or nod.

"Mario, come up here for a second. Let's try out some of the things we've been talking about. What if I saw you in the hall and I said to you in a real loud voice, 'What are you looking at, hater?' What would you do?"

"I'd just walk away, man. I don't have time for that game."

"Good thinking, Mario. Now, the rest of you were in the hallway when I confronted Mario and saw him walk away. Which of us looks like a loser? Me or Mario?"

"You do!" the students say.

"Exactly! Mario comes out looking like a winner. Now do you think you guys can do some of the things we've been talking about when you're out in the hallways? Think about what we've talked about, and how you can take some positive control when somebody insults you. We're going to visit about this at the end of the week, so be ready to share some stories about what you saw and did in the hallways, okay?"

Another student, Shonna, who has been sitting quietly, now says, "Nobody better never front on me like that. They'll get served with the quickness."

Ms. Tucker responds: "Well, if you feel like you have to serve somebody here at school and not choose one of the better options, then that's on you. Just know you've got options and that we're here for you. Cool?"

"Cool," says Shonna.

"This has been a great discussion!" the teacher says. "Because you worked hard on this today, you all get a two-day extension on your book reports. They'll be due on Thursday next week rather than Tuesday."

Let's look at the components of Proactive Teaching, using the scenario above.

▶ **Introduce the skill and discuss it with students:** Give a general explanation of the skill, and the different ways it can be used, and then outline the specific steps that make up the skill. By describing different ways to use the skill, you can help students generalize the behavior. Be specific about the steps that make up the skill and about your expectations for accomplishing those steps.

In the example, the skill under discussion was how to keep your cool if you're insulted. The teacher drew her students into a lengthy discussion about what happens when the skill is not used and how the hallways and cafeteria could be safer if more people resisted the impulse to fight when they faced an insult or accusation from another student.

It's always a plus to have students generate the components of the skill you're discussing, to have them describe how the skill looks to them. If students have input, they will feel more ownership of the skill and will be more likely to use it. Of course, you have to make certain that student input doesn't create a situation that runs afoul of district or school policies.

▶ **Give a reason and talk about it:** List a variety of benefits or payoffs that may come from using the new skill. Have students help formulate ideas. The benefits or payoffs, called rationales, should be reasons that hit youngsters where they live. For example, it's a lot easier to convince teenagers that they will have more friends if they learn to disagree appropriately, rather than using the rationale that the skill will come in handy when they find themselves negotiating a deal in the business world.

Long-term rationales are not as effective as short-term rationales, because kids want to see immediate results for their efforts. Long-term rationales do work, however, once young people learn a skill because they can then see how the skill will benefit them in the future.

As you talk about rationales with students, get their ideas about what they see as valuable in the skill you're discussing. Ask them if their friends value the skill in the same way and if they have a sense of how their families would value the skill. Getting these different perspectives will give you a better sense of how the skill is likely to fit in the student's world and how you can best motivate him or her to embrace the skill.

In the story we just reviewed, the teacher asked students to discuss the reasoning behind the skill, and she gave them a student-centered reason for using the skill: the fact that they would be less likely to have a reputation as a troublemaker if they resisted the temptation to fight in the hallways.

▶ **Request acknowledgment:** This is as simple as saying, "Do you understand?" or "Does that make sense?" Including this step allows you to determine whether students are following your teaching. In the story, the teacher checked with her students to see if they understood what she was saying and she also asked a lot of questions, both to see if they were following her and to engage them in the process of learning the new skill.

▶ **Practice:** This step actively involves students in brief role-plays and demonstrations. Or you may suggest that students try the new skill in a "real world" setting and report their experiences later to you. The teacher in the example used both types of practice.

If you are practicing a complex skill or what to do in a difficult situation, never promise that the situation will work out perfectly. Remind your students that they are practicing possible ways to handle a situation and that the outcome won't always be the same as the one that's practiced. But they will feel better because they at least have thought about the situation and have examined one possible outcome.

If you've asked students to practice a skill outside the classroom, be sure to check back with them and have a discussion about what their experiences were, so you can determine whether you need to do more teaching. These "real life" practices are beneficial because they help students generalize behavior to other settings.

▶ **Give a positive consequence:** You may want to give your students a positive consequence for their cooperation in Proactive Teaching. In the example, the teacher allowed her students an extra two days on their book reports because of their lively participation in the class discussion.

Determining consequences is generally easy when working with an individual student, but somewhat more difficult when teaching a large group. Group consequences must be carefully selected to make sure the reinforcement is contingent upon everyone's performance.

It's important to emphasize to students how valuable their participation is to a group discussion. You can encourage participation by randomly calling on students or going around the room and having everyone offer a comment on the discussion. You also can encourage participation by making the payoff significantly enticing to students.

◆ Variations

As with other teaching in the Boys Town Education Model, Proactive Teaching is flexible. You can effectively use the concepts in your classroom without using every single step. Following is an example of a variation of Proactive Teaching. As you become familiar with Proactive Teaching, you will be able to develop your own variations.

▶ **Introduce and explore the skill and give a rationale:** *"Next week, you'll be taking the state achievement tests, so we're going to talk a bit today about preparing for those tests. Have you all taken these tests before?"*

The students nod.

"Great, then you know the drill. What are some of the things you must have to take the test?"

"Those famous Number 2 pencils," laughs one student.

"That's right. Remember to sharpen them before the test, so you'll be ready to go. Now when you answer the questions on this test, you have to fill in those little ovals. What does that mean, Valerie?"

"You have to press hard and fill in the oval all the way, or your answer won't count."

"Good description. And remember the tests are timed, so you have to stay focused. If you come prepared and stay on task, you'll do great on the tests and they really will reflect how hard you've been working and studying. Does that make sense?" The teacher looks around the

classroom and sees students nodding and showing her the "thumbs up" sign, which her class uses to show they understand. "Great," she says, "Then let's get back to 'Othello.'"

◆ Monitoring and Supervision

We've been discussing Proactive Teaching mostly in the context of classroom settings, but you also will find the teaching method useful when you're outside the classroom – standing in your doorway during passing period, for example – or on cafeteria duty.

Studies have shown that areas like hallways, cafeterias, and playgrounds are prime locations for violent encounters, and experts urge teachers to extend their teaching to students in these areas, in an effort to reclaim ownership of their schools and reduce violence.

When you move from a classroom setting to a hallway or cafeteria, obviously the topics you're addressing with students will change, but you'll still be using the basic skill of providing teaching to help a student avoid a problem or to keep a situation from escalating into trouble.

The assistant principal is on his way to the office during classes, and he sees two students standing beside an open locker. "Hey guys, what's up?" the assistant principal asks. "Where are you guys supposed to be right now?" The students say they're on their way to third-period English class, so the assistant principal waits until they retrieve a book and then walks them to class.

In this example, the assistant principal has observed students in a place where they're not supposed to be – in the hallway during classes. He questions why they are there, and he remains with them until they return to their classroom. The purpose of his Proactive Teaching is to guide the students from a potentially precarious setting – the hallway – to one where they can be safe and successful – their regular classroom.

The assistant principal's actions in the hallway can be easily divided into two components – monitoring and supervision.

The monitoring portion of his action was to take notice of youngsters who weren't where they were supposed to be.

The supervision portion occurred when the assistant principal asked questions of the students, determined where they were headed, and accompanied them to their destination.

When you do Proactive Teaching in hallways, cafeterias, and other non-academic settings, keep the elements of monitoring and supervision in mind. And remember that nonacademic Proactive Teaching is rooted in the same concepts as the classroom variety. In the same way a teacher uses Proactive Teaching to direct Journalism I students in a successful discussion about using quotes, the assistant principal is using Proactive Teaching to successfully direct the wayward students back to their classroom.

Here are some tips for using Proactive Teaching in nonacademic settings. Keep in mind that some of these ideas also may come in handy in the classroom:

- Listen to what students are saying. Know their slang so you'll understand what they're talking about.

- Watch what students do. Be aware of body language.
- Check on their whereabouts.
- Ask questions: "Where are you going now?" "What are you doing?"
- Show them you're watching: "Where's that hat belong, Jimmy?" "No running, Claire." "Nice game last night, Pete." "Good job on announcements today, Eric."

A teacher is standing outside his classroom during passing period and he sees two sophomore boys roughhousing in the hall, jostling other students as they take fake punches at each other. The teacher speaks up: "Marcus, Donnie, settle down. This isn't WWF."

Again, we can see that Proactive Teaching is a tool for teachers to use to direct students to do the right thing. In the example above, the teacher warns the boys against their roughhousing, which could escalate into more serious behavior, but the teacher uses a touch of humor to soften his warning a bit, reminding the teenagers that the school isn't a stop on the World Wrestling Federation tour.

In both this example and the earlier one about the assistant principal escorting students back to the classroom from the hallway, it may seem like the adults were correcting students. So why is this Proactive Teaching? Because the goal of both adults is to *prevent* further problems. Kids will test the limits of the rules. Adults who actively remind students of the boundaries prevent behavior from getting out of hand.

◆ Code-Switching

None of us lives in one world. We all move regularly between worlds, and as we move, the rules change. We follow different behavioral rules at work, for example, than we do when we're at home relaxing with a group of friends.

An important component of Proactive Teaching is showing young people how to move successfully and safely from one world to another, adopting the correct set of behaviors as they move. We call this process "code-switching."

When teenagers successfully learn to switch codes, they know when to use a greeting of "Whassup, man?" and when to say "Good morning, Mr. Tatum." They know that they can playfully give a teacher a hard time during class, but not when the principal is observing. They know what words to choose to keep them safe on the streets of their neighborhood and what words are acceptable in the hallways at school.

Code-switching is a particularly useful skill for teenagers who come from at-risk environments. These youngsters often haven't learned to read the behavioral cues of a traditional school setting. Because they lack these socialization skills, they often feel alienated at school and see the school environment as punishing.

For example, many teenagers and sometimes younger kids regularly use swear words in their casual conversations at their regular hangouts – the mall, movies, restaurants, or while they're playing video games. Using that language is normal, accepted behavior in their peer group.

But a teenager can't hurl a robust "F---, dude!" when someone steps on his foot in the library or say "I can't get this damned computer to print" in the computer lab.

When young people learn code-switching, they see the different expectations of the different environments they move between. Because they learn about the different expectations, they know what is expected of them, and they can more handily meet the requirements of the setting. The result is more successful interactions and a reduction in their negative feelings, creating more of an opportunity to learn.

Here are some tips for teaching your students how to code-switch:

▶ **Discuss the different settings they will find themselves in:** school, work, church, a friend's house, a party, a dark street at night.

▶ **Discuss what behaviors are expected in each setting**: sit up straight and pay attention in school, relax and chat at a party.

▶ **Discuss what to do if they find themselves in an unfamiliar setting:** how to observe others' behaviors as a clue to what is expected; how to know whether others are doing the right thing in a situation.

As students grow more skilled at code-switching, they will gradually learn to feel more comfortable in new situations and they will have learned a repertoire of skills that they can draw on to make them feel at ease.

◆ Benefits of Proactive Teaching

Proactive Teaching can enhance your effectiveness as a teacher because you can set clear expectations for student behavior. Through "up-front" teaching, you can establish and demonstrate tolerance levels and consequences. You can model these expectations as you teach skills and communicate the importance of skill-building through repeated instruction and feedback. You also can keep a strong focus on individual goals for students.

Proactive Teaching also increases the opportunities for students to learn. By gaining their input, having them practice skills in "safe" situations, and giving feedback to others, you provide students many chances to participate in the learning process. And they may acquire skills more quickly because lessons are presented at a neutral time, which may help them be more open to feedback on their performance.

Proactive Teaching also builds solid relationships between teachers and students. The entire process demonstrates respect, concern, and fairness. Practice sessions and positive consequences build student confidence and provide alternative behaviors for students who previously relied on aggressive or other negative behaviors.

◆ When to Use Proactive Teaching

Proactive Teaching can be used to teach basic or advanced skills, to prepare students for specific situations or circumstances, and in individualized teaching. Although the most logical time to use Proactive Teaching may seem like the beginning of a new school year, it can and should be used whenever a need arises, such as discussing fighting in the hallways or preparing your class for a substitute teacher.

When students are prepared to deal with the situations life throws at them, they feel safe, and that leaves them more open to learning. Because of that, they are more likely to experience success in school and to view school as a positive place.

Chapter Summary

Proactive Teaching: Is a way to prevent problems by telling students what to do and having them practice before they encounter a specific situation.

Use when students are learning something new, or when they have had difficulty in a past situation.

"Up-front teaching" clearly outlines expectations, builds student confidence.

Can be used to teach social skills or academics.

Types of Proactive Teaching

Planned Teaching: Teaching students a new skill or reviewing a skill previously taught. Example: All-school assembly on fire safety.

Preventive Prompt: A brief reminder to students to behave in a way they have been taught. Example: "Steve, remember to be on time tomorrow, or you'll have your third tardy and have to do a detention."

Components of Proactive Teaching

Introduce the skill; discuss with students

Give a reason to use the skill; discuss with students

Request acknowledgment

Practice

Positive Consequence

Variations

Outside the Classroom: Monitoring and Supervision

Keeping hallways, commons, cafeterias safe.

Monitoring: Noticing what students are doing and where they are.

Supervision: Talking with students about what they are doing, where they are supposed to be.

Code-switching: Teaching students to adopt the correct set of behaviors to the setting they find themselves in.

Benefits of Proactive Teaching

Establishes tolerance levels and consequences

Increases learning opportunities by building self-confidence

Builds relationships between students and teachers

When to Use Proactive Teaching

To teach basic or advanced skills

To prepare for specific situations, circumstances

In individualized teaching

Chapter Ten

Self-Control for Students

The punch not thrown or the curse unspoken are powerful testaments to self-control for the student who once relied on aggressive and violent behaviors to make it through the day.

But it is not just the most aggressive or violent students who benefit from taking control of their thoughts, feelings, and behaviors. This life skill is essential to all students, for it is a fundamental tool for living in society.

In this chapter, we will review some basic self-control strategies used at Boys Town. While much of our discussion will refer to using these strategies with aggressive youth, the methods also work well with other youth who occasionally have trouble keeping their tempers in check.

◆ Strategies for Self-Control

Aggressive and antisocial youth often are highly agitated, a behavior that frequently leads them into conflict not only with adults, but also their peers (Walker, Colvin, & Ramsey, 1995).

These youth carry intense levels of anger, and sometimes rage. Some act out because they have been abused. In addition, they carry feelings of alienation, and many have great difficulty controlling and managing their anger effectively. Most have not been taught appropriate ways to control their angry feelings (Walker, Colvin, & Ramsey, 1995).

In fact, the tantrums, confrontations, and other inappropriate behaviors they use when they're angry usually work well for these youngsters. They have learned that when they accelerate these behaviors, other people back away, allowing them to have their way in many situations. Because of this, it's often difficult for these students to replace the inappropriate behaviors with appropriate ones; it's hard to abandon something that works (Walker, Colvin, & Ramsey, 1995).

But they must replace these behaviors with anger control strategies that are socially acceptable. They must learn to recognize the situations that trigger an angry response in them, and they must realize what the consequences are for their inappropriate responses.

Boys Town youth use the strategies outlined in this chapter to help regain control of their behaviors. Each youth is assigned three self-control strategies because one strategy may work better than others in certain settings and situations.

To begin teaching these strategies, start your teaching session at a time when the student is calm and not misbehaving. This is when the youth should be most receptive to your instruction. You can use the principles of Proactive Teaching to instruct students in these principles. Proactive Teaching may be used with individual students or in a group classroom setting.

Next, identify a self-control strategy from the following list and give examples of how and when it could be used. For example, positive self-talk could be used when the student is in class and it's not convenient to excuse himself and find a quiet place. The student could use writing or drawing in a journal at home.

Once you've outlined where the strategies can be put to use, describe for the student the steps of each strategy. Demonstrate if necessary. Then, give the student some reasons for using the strategy. You might point out, for example, that using one of the self-control strategies might help the student control his temper and avoid earning a consequence.

As you teach, ask the student if he or she understands what you are saying. Then, have the youngster practice using the strategy in a pretend situation. Give the youth feedback on the practice and reinforce him or her for practicing.

A student who learns two or three of these strategies and gets good at using them is more likely to respond to upsetting situations in a calm and positive manner. Here are the strategies and how to use them:

▶ Deep-Breathing

- Silently count to five as you take a deep breath in through your nose.

- Hold the breath for five seconds.

- Count to five again as you let the breath out slowly through your mouth.

- Take two normal breaths.

- Repeat the first three steps two or three times until you feel yourself calming down.

- When you are calm, tell an adult.

▶ Writing or Drawing in a Journal

- Go some place where you won't be disturbed.

- Write down (or draw a picture that shows) how you are feeling and what you are thinking.

- When you are calm, tell an adult.

▶ Take Time to Cool Down

- Go someplace where you won't be disturbed or distracted.

- Take five minutes to calm down.

- If you need more time, calmly ask for it.

- When you are calm, tell an adult.

▶ Positive Self-Talk

- Make a positive comment about how you can handle a situation appropriately. Use a phrase such as "I can get myself under control"; "I've done it before, I can do it

Anger Inventory

Circle the answer below that best describes your situation.

Where did the incident occur?

Classroom Commons

P.E. Class Bathroom

Lunchroom Off Campus

What happened?

Unable to listen to teacher Refused to do something

Argued with another student I did something wrong

Other_____

What did you do?

Raised my voice Walked away calmly

Used inappropriate language Threw something

Hit someone Attempted to use proper social skills

Other _____

How did you handle yourself?

Poorly Not good

Okay Good

Great

How angry were you?

Mad as I can be Really angry

Moderately angry Mildly angry but still okay

Not angry

How would I handle this situation differently if it happened again? *(Fill in the blank)*

_____

_____

_____

_____

again"; "If I stop now, things will get better"; or "I can do this."

- Repeat the statement you choose until you are calm.

- When you are calm, tell an adult.

▶ Visualization

- Picture yourself calm.

- Picture yourself in a favorite place, such as in a quiet forest or on a beach.

- Picture yourself doing something you enjoy, such as listening to your favorite music.

▶ Muscle Relaxation

- Clench and squeeze your fists for five seconds, and slowly release them.

- Slowly roll your neck in circles for five seconds.

- Scrunch your shoulders and slowly roll them in circles several times.

- Slowly rotate your ankles.

- Raise your eyebrows as high as you can and then slowly lower them.

- Scrunch your face and release.

- When you are calm, tell an adult.

To help students recognize what makes them upset and what happens when they start to feel that way, observe their behaviors. For example, if you notice that a student always gets angry when someone teases him and that he starts breathing faster just before he blows up, you can explain this to him. Then you can teach him a self-control strategy like those listed here. Eventually, he will learn to recognize the situation (teasing) and the signal (breathing faster) and know that he can choose an appropriate way to respond.

Keep in mind that there are many self-control strategies available. Some of the best ones are those you create to address problems with specific students. One urban school that was having trouble with gangs developed a "Pledge for Peace" program for students.

Students in the program signed contracts (the Pledge for Peace) where they promised to promote nonviolence in their classroom and the building by using a particular life skill, such as self-control. The contract included a form that each student completed, explaining how that life skill will promote peace.

Another method to help students is an "Anger Inventory." The inventory, which students complete after they have lost self control, helps students pinpoint the emotional and environmental factors that may have come together to spark their anger. (See the example on page 103.)

The inventory, completed when a student has calmed down, may help the youth gain insight into situations that trigger aggressive behaviors and help him or her in the future.

◆ Suggestions for Maintaining Control

Being able to express feelings honestly is a key to remaining in control. These tips have suggestions for how to identify and focus feelings.

▶ Anger Control

Listen to what is being said to you.
Monitor your body and breathing.
Tell yourself to breathe slowly and deeply.
Relax tense body areas.
Ask for a few minutes alone if
    you need that.
While alone, continue to relax.

▶ **Expressing Feelings**

Remain calm and relaxed.
Describe how you are feeling.
Avoid blaming.
Take responsibility for your feelings.
Thank others for listening.

Some students use the following "self-talk" strategies when they seem to be losing self-control; others try to focus on using the following assertive behaviors instead of aggression.

▶ **Self-Talk Strategies**

STOP what you are doing if it is causing a problem.
LOOK at what is happening around you.
THINK of a better choice.
TELL yourself to make that choice.
REWARD yourself for making a good choice.

▶ **Assertiveness Strategies**

LOOK at the other person.
SPEAK in a calm voice.
STAY relaxed and breathe deeply.
STATE your opinion clearly.
AVOID emotional terms.
LISTEN to other views.

▶ **Conflict Resolution Strategies**

Approach the situation calmly and rationally.
Listen to others involved.
Express your feelings.
Acknowledge other points of view.
Express willingness to negotiate to compromise.
Arrive at a mutually beneficial resolution.

Working with students to develop self-control and problem-solving skills can be a lengthy process filled with frustration. Dealing with students whose anger takes them from a detention to a suspension within a matter of minutes can be a heartbreaking experience.

But teaching youth to use self-control strategies and good problem-solving to make mature decisions is a rewarding experience. That kind of success can reinforce the very best part of teaching – the ability to shape a young person's future.

Chapter Summary

Self-Control Strategies

Deep-Breathing
Writing or Drawing in a Journal
Take Time to Cool Down
Positive Self-Talk
Visualization
Muscle Relaxation

Anger Inventory

Suggestions for Maintaining Control

Anger Control
Expressing Feelings
Self-Talk Strategies
Assertiveness Strategies
Conflict Resolution Strategies

Chapter Eleven

Problem-Solving and Goal-Setting

As students learn about the connections between their thoughts, feelings, and behaviors, and gradually begin to take control of their lives, they will be ready to tackle problem-solving and goal-setting, two skills that they will use throughout their lives. The skills are similar in that they require analysis, plus the ability to formulate an action plan and perseverance to complete the plan. Let's take an in-depth look at both skills.

◆ Problem-Solving Strategies

Remember the old adage: "Give a man a fish, and he can eat for a day; teach a man to fish, and he will eat for a lifetime,"? It's the same way with teaching youth problem-solving strategies. You could spend your whole day solving students' problems for them, but, as a teacher, you can better serve your students by giving them tools they can use to solve their own problems. With those tools, they have skills for a lifetime.

Students can use problem-solving strategies to resolve conflicts, plan for the future, and make decisions about how they will live their lives. Many difficulties that youth have develop as a result of their poor decision-making. Problem-solving skills can help youngsters learn to clearly think through an issue before making a decision.

Teaching problem-solving skills also can be an effective way to build relationships with students. As you help students work through problems, they will see that you respect their confidences and are concerned and helpful. They, in turn, will feel more comfortable with you and gain confidence in their abilities.

Teaching problem-solving is most effective when a student is calm and focused and needs to develop a plan to deal with a challenge he or she is facing. The challenge may be one that the student is currently experiencing or one that he or she is anticipating, such as talking with a teacher about an exam grade, resisting peer pressure, or deciding whether to participate in a school activity.

You also can use problem-solving techniques to follow up after Corrective or Crisis Teaching as a way to teach the student how to cope in the future.

Sometimes, students just need someone to listen to them. When they've had a bad day or are experiencing personal or family difficulties, young people just want to let someone know how they feel. You may eventually use problem-solving strategies to help the student cope with the difficulty, but listening should be your first priority.

Also keep in mind that the problems some youth face will require you to take action beyond helping them explore solutions. For example, sexual abuse, sexual harassment, evidence of involvement in a crime – all must be reported to authorities. You still will be able to lend support to the student, but your first priority will be to alert the proper school district and legal authorities to take necessary action.

But for situations that don't require that level of attention, you will be able to help your students learn how to analyze and solve problems by breaking them down into their component parts. We call this the POP method.

◆ Solving Problems with POP

POP is an acronym that stands for the following steps:

P: Define the **problem.**

O: Examine **options** to solve the problem, and then list the disadvantages and advantages of the options.

P: Decide on a **plan** of action to solve the problem.

Usually, POP discussions involve sitting down with a student and having him or her use a pen and paper to write down ideas for each step. Having the student write out his or her version of the situation is important because that will give you an idea of how the student is viewing the problem. In addition, the process of writing down ideas is important because it forces kids to be deliberate and thoughtful rather than impulsive. And having the ideas in writing allows you to review them as you and the student decide on the best solution to the problem.

A discussion of each step follows.

▶ **Problem:** The problem-solving process begins with you helping the student to clearly define the situation or problem. In some cases, the student may give vague or emotional descriptions, such as "I'm sick of school." By asking open-ended questions, such as "Can you explain that some more?", you may be able to help the youth more fully describe the situation. However, you may have to ask more direct questions (e.g., "Why are you sick of school?") to get to the root or cause. Be sure to infuse your questioning with empathy, concern, and encouragement to draw out the student. Without this concern, your questions may sound like an interrogation, and that could cause him or her to withdraw.

As the student more clearly defines the problem, it's your job to summarize what the youngster is saying. Sometimes, the problem is easy to identify; other times it will take awhile.

When the student agrees with your summary, you should have a pretty accurate picture of the situation and the scope of the problem. If your summary is inaccurate or incomplete, tell the student that he or she should correct you.

Summarizing the problem correctly is important since the rest of the process depends upon this step.

▶ **Options:** After the problem is clearly defined, ask the student to write down possible options for solving it. Be careful not to pass judgment on any option the youth suggests; this can be difficult, especially when a student suggests one that would only make matters worse, such as beating up someone. Remember that your role at this point is to get the youth to generate options. Think of this step as simple brainstorming.

You can help the student generate options, but don't offer your ideas until the student has run out of ideas of his or her own. Then, offer your ideas in the form of a question, such as "How about talking to the teacher after class?", so the student stays involved in the process. Over time, students will get better at generating options.

After the student has developed at least three viable options, help him or her make a list of disadvantages and advantages for each one. This process helps the student see the cause-and-effect relationship between decisions and what happens to him or her.

As in generating options, it is important to have the student think through the disadvantages and advantages. Your role is to skillfully guide the student by asking general questions, such as "Can you think of any problems that might occur if you do that?" If the youth has difficulty thinking of disadvantages and advantages, make your questions more specific (e.g., "Well, what do you think your teacher would do if you started a fight in class?"). Try to solicit as many disadvantages and advantages as possible from the student.

Continue to remain nonjudgmental as the student comes up with disadvantages and advantages. When a student seems enthusiastic about the advantages of an option that is not realistic, ask questions that help the student see the negative side of the option. For example, if a student thinks it would be great to fight a classmate who's been picking on him, you could ask your student what might happen if he lost the fight or got hurt.

If the youth clearly does not see or can't be directed to offer an important advantage or disadvantage, you can offer your viewpoint and allow the student to react to it.

After you've discussed the disadvantages and advantages of all the options, summarize the pros and cons of each option. This summary helps the youth see the cause-and-effect relationship more clearly.

Then have the student select what he or she thinks is the best option. You may have to point out more disadvantages yourself to help the student see what the best option is.

▶ **Plan:** This step involves having the student select a plan of attack to solve the problem. It also can include role-play sessions to help the student prepare to execute his or her plan.

When the youth selects his or her option, it may not always be the best option from your point of view. But it is more important that it be the option the student chooses. The youngster is more likely to be committed to make an option work if he or she is truly comfortable with it and feels ownership of the choice.

After the student has selected an option, you should offer reassurance that he or she can make it work. This will make the student comfortable with the choice. Answer any questions the student has about how to successfully implement the option. This is also a good time to set up a role-play or practice, which can help the student gain confidence in the option. Try to make the role-play as realistic as possible.

As a teacher, you'll probably know the people the student will interact with as he or she implements the solution. They could be parents, friends, employers, the principal, or other instructors. If you know the people involved, you can respond as you think they might. For example, if the principal at your school is fairly abrupt and somewhat stern, portray her in that manner during the role-play. You also can make the role-play more realistic by giving the student several possible responses. This should make the student more comfortable with what's likely to happen.

Be encouraging! Praise the student for thinking of a plan to handle the problem. Ask some "what if" questions (e.g. "What are you going to do if this happens?"). Ask the student to check back with you after he or she takes action on the plan. Offer praise if the option works. If not, be empathetic and supportive, and offer to do another POP to find out what went wrong and then come up with a more successful solution.

◆ Other Problem-Solving Techniques

POP is an effective problem-solving tool, but don't neglect opportunities to discuss other ways to solve problems. The more tools students have, the more likely they are to choose an appropriate method over an inappropriate method.

Classroom discussion on an academic topic, for example, may provide a forum to teach problem-solving. In a history class, for example, discussion about why a nation went to war may prompt another discussion on what options the country had to avoid war and what other decisions it might have made. Your literature class could discuss problem-solving as you examine actions a character takes in a book the class is reading.

On page 111 and 112 are two POP forms. One is blank and can be reproduced for your students to use. The other form is completed with a sample problem analysis.

◆ Setting Goals

Often, youth who rely on aggressive and violent behaviors aren't very good at planning for the future. They live in the moment. They don't have a plan for getting their English project finished, or graduating, or finding a way to make a living. As a result, these youth often drift through school and life, feeling no real sense of accomplishment in anything because they have not bothered to invest any time or effort into setting goals for themselves.

The key to teaching these students how to set goals is to show them that goal-setting is a way to take control of a situation and work toward getting the things they want. For many students, that can be a very attractive incentive.

One method to teach students about goal-setting is to have each of them write down a goal he or she would like to achieve, then brainstorm the steps the student thinks will have to be taken to achieve that goal.

For this exercise, students may choose any goal. Some may be very concrete, such as buying a car. Others may be less so, such as becoming a TV star. Consider having students write down their goals and accompanying steps separately, then come together as a class to discuss the steps. This discussion will help students shape the expectations they have and determine what steps they must take to meet their goals. Then they can develop a realistic idea of what is

Solving Problems with POP
(Problem • Options • Plan)

Problem

Describe your problem here:

Options

Make a list of ways you could solve the problem. Then list some advantages and disadvantages of each option:

Option #1:

Advantages:

Disadvantages:

Option #2:

Advantages:

Disadvantages:

Option #3:

Advantages:

Disadvantages:

Plan

Decide which option will work best to solve the problem. Briefly describe how you will put your plan to work to solve the problem.

Solving Problems with POP
(Problem • Options • Plan)

Problem

Describe your problem here: I want to try out for the school play, but I have a part-time job after school. I'm afraid I couldn't get the time off to make the practices.

Options

Make a list of ways you could solve the problem. Then list some advantages and disadvantages of each option:

Option #1: I could quit my job.

Advantages: I would have plenty of time for the play and other stuff after school. I would have more time to spend with my friends. I would have more time to do my homework.

Disadvantages: I wouldn't have any money. I wouldn't get to see my friends at work. I wouldn't get to list work experience on my college applications. I wouldn't have work experience for future jobs.

Option #2: I could talk to my boss about changing my hours so I could try out for the play.

Advantages: I could maybe keep my job and still do the play. Aleysha could work some extra hours; she's been wanting more hours anyway.

Disadvantages: My boss might get mad if I try to cut my hours. He might fire me.

Option #3: I could go ahead and try out for the play. If I get a part, then I'll talk to my boss.

Advantages: If I don't get a part, then I don't have to bug my boss about getting time off. I will know more about the practice schedule after I've been through tryouts.

Disadvantages: What happens if I get a part, but then can't get the time off? Then I'm letting down the rest of the cast.

Plan

Decide which option will work best to solve the problem. Briefly describe how you will put your plan to work to solve the problem.

I'll talk to my boss first and tell him I'm thinking about trying out for the play and ask him what the possibilities are for changing my schedule. I can talk to the drama teacher before I talk to my boss, so I can get a general idea about what the play's practice schedule is. If I can't get my work schedule changed, I will skip the play. I really do need my job.

actually involved in reaching a goal like buying a used car or starring in a situation comedy on television.

You can use the following information to help students do the exercise and begin thinking about goal-setting.

◆ Goal-Setting: A Lesson for Students

▶ Steps to Establishing Goals

G – Decide what **goal** you want to get.

O – **Organize** your options.

A – Take **action** in small steps; **ask** for help.

L – **Look** over your plan and results.

S – **Seek** alternatives and adjust as necessary.

▶ Decide what goal you want to get:

The first step in goal-setting is to determine what you want your future to look like. This is where you fill in the blank: "I want _____." You might be answering with "a new car," "a spring break vacation next year," "an M.D. after my name," or many other wishes.

In this step, you must clearly identify what you want. It's not good enough to say "I want to be famous," or "I want to be happy." Although those are noble goals, they are not specific enough for anyone to act on. For one person, being famous might mean having a worldwide identity, such as Princess Diana. Somebody else might decide that being the town mayor means being famous. For one person, being happy may mean finding a cure for cancer, but another person who seeks happiness might want to write poetry in a tiny cabin by the ocean.

The point is to be as specific as you can in defining your goal. Shut your eyes and picture yourself accomplishing your goal. What do you see? If you see yourself happily scribbling away in that cabin by the ocean, then you will want to find a way to make that specific vision a reality. How will you learn about poetry? What kind of poetry will you write? What is your cabin going to look like? How much can you afford to spend on it? What ocean will you be near? Answering all those questions is where the remaining steps in the process come in.

▶ Organize your options:

Suppose your goal is getting a car that you can use to drive yourself to school and to work. That's a pretty clear goal, but you still have some work to do to define what steps you need to take to get those wheels. Now you must figure out what kind of car you want and, more specifically, what kind of car you can afford.

To organize your options, you may want to make some lists. The first list could be a "wish list" of all the great cars you wish you could have. This will be fun, but you'll know from the outset that you probably can't afford most of the vehicles on this first list.

So make a second list after you take a look at your bank account. Once you know how much money you have to spend, you can start looking at the classified ads in your newspaper to see what cars listed are in your price range. This will give you an idea of the make and model of vehicle you can afford.

Another list you might make are ways to finance your new car if you don't have enough money in your bank account to pay for the car all at once. Can your parents loan you some money? Can you get a loan at your bank? Would you be able to finance the vehicle another way, such as making weekly payments to the car dealer? Now you're ready to gather up those lists and get to work.

▶ **Take action in small steps; ask for help:** Now that you have lists of things to do, you can begin your car search in earnest. You may want to attack your list of financial concerns first, in order to be sure you have money to pay for the vehicle you want. Then you can start visiting car lots or calling about cars you see listed in the newspaper classifieds. As you start checking items off your list, you will likely narrow your search down to several alternative choices. You'll probably have many questions as you arrange financing and travel around town to look at cars. Don't be afraid to ask questions to make sure you have all the information you need to make an informed choice.

▶ **Look over your plan and results:** At this point, you're ready to make a choice on your new car. When you get to this step, you'll be doing some of the same activities as in problem-solving, including making a list of advantages and disadvantages and weighing those against each other to determine the best decision.

▶ **Seek alternatives and adjust as necessary:** In this final step, you will look for alternatives if the plan you've developed isn't working out. Say, for example, that you have narrowed your car list down to a nice, clean coupe you saw on a dealer's lot, but when you go back to buy it, the car's been sold. Because of this, you'll have to choose the number two car on your list, or perhaps start your search again, organizing your options, taking action, and looking over your plan once more. Don't be discouraged if this happens. Sometimes these things happen for the best. Maybe you'll end up with a better deal than what you had with your first plan. Or maybe you'll just have to hitch a ride with your buddy for another couple of weeks until you find a substitute car. Just hang in there and work the steps to meet your goal.

Learning to systematically solve problems and set goals can be a life-transforming experience for a student. Not only do students learn a skill they can always use, they also get a sense of accomplishment for tackling a complex issue without resorting to violence or aggression to make things turn out their way. And that sense of accomplishment is a powerful reinforcement in a young life.

Chapter Summary

Problem-Solving Strategies

    Solving Problems with POP

        Problem

        Options

        Plan

    Other Problem-Solving Techniques

Setting Goals

    Step-by-Step

        Decide what goal you want to get

        Organize your options

        Take action in small steps; ask for help

        Look over your plan and results

        Seek alternatives and adjust as necessary

ChapterTwelve

A Safe Place to Learn

Welcome to Anywhere High School. It's your first visit. You're a member of an evaluation team that is assessing safety at this and other district schools. You decide to take a stroll around the building as the first bell rings, signaling the beginning of the school day.

Near the school office, the principal and two vice-principals are in the hallways, greeting students and monitoring for the presence of pager or dress code violations.

Students enter the building through the front doors because other doors around the building are locked. The kids move toward their lockers, which are covered with graffiti and marred by rust. At their lockers, students hang up jackets, grab their books, and begin the stroll to class.

As you move through the hallways with the students, you see some teachers out in the halls, greeting students, discussing the latest football game, and encouraging the young people to get to class on time. Other teachers are busy in their classrooms, reviewing lesson plans or punching

grades into the computer as the throng of students piles up at the doors of classrooms.

The warning bell rings and the pace in the hallways picks up. Kids shove each other through cramped doorways to avoid tardies, while other students begin to run to class. The security guard, relaxing in his favorite corner, yells at a group of students, reminding them to slow down.

You see a student slip out a side door, leaving it open a crack; another student immediately enters. You watch as that student heads to the attendance office to get a late pass. Meanwhile, you see another youngster – probably a sophomore – come barreling into the attendance office. She yells at the clerk to give her a pass. The clerk, unshaken by the loud demand, stoically writes up both a late pass and a detention, which is the consequence for being tardy.

As you step into a math classroom, it seems quiet. Students are supposed to be working problems in their workbooks, but you see a note being passed from one student to another, and a boy in the back rhythmically drumming a pencil on the shoulder of the boy in front of him. Two girls on the other side of the room are looking at the latest issue of People magazine. Throughout the room, students have their feet on the backs of other students' chairs. The teacher sits at her desk, head down, grading papers.

In the English class down the hall, you hear the low buzz of students working in small groups while others practice presentations that they will give tomorrow. The teacher wanders from group to group, answering questions and offering suggestions.

When the bell rings for lunch, students rush to the doors of their classrooms and make a mad beeline for the cafeteria. In the lunch room, you see the monitors stroll in after all the students are in the cafeteria. The kids form a rowdy, ragtag chow line. The noise in the cafeteria is hair-raising. Students yell at each other across the cavernous room.

The monitors walk around, talking to students about their activities, classes, and the Homecoming dance next week. The monitors occasionally ask a student to quiet down. After about 15 minutes of walking around, the monitors gather against one wall, where they spend the rest of the lunch hour chatting. When the bell rings, students head back to class, leaving trash and lunch trays on the tables for the cleaning crew to pick up.

Outside the cafeteria, you stop to look at the trophy case, which displays honors that students have received for academic and sports accomplishments. On a long wall nearby are all kinds of posters cheering on the football team and urging attendance at the Homecoming dance.

As the day draws to a close in mid-afternoon, announcements crackle over the intercom.

Everyone stops to listen, but some of the intercom speakers need repair, and the announcements are hard to decipher in some classrooms.

When the dismissal bell rings, you notice that some walls in the hallway look dingy, and on some, you can even make out the impressions of fingerprints and handprints. You stop to get a drink of water at a water fountain, but it's not working.

Some teachers holler goodbye to students, and you see other teachers walking down the halls, talking to kids. After about 10 minutes, the hallways are quiet, but other parts of the building are a whirl of activity. You can hear volleyballs bouncing in the gym, and in the auditorium, a student is practicing a song for the upcoming musical while other students hammer nails into a set. Outside, the football coach's whistle rings out over the practice field, and the marching band is having fun with its rendition of "The Pink Panther Theme."

The scenario above is a pretty typical example of an average day in an American high school. Anywhere High School is probably a lot like your school, and, like your school, it has made some strides in making itself a safer place to learn. But as we've seen tragically in American communities such as Littleton, Colo., Springfield, Ore., and Jonesboro, Ark., there is much work still to do.

Let's review some of the positive efforts we saw on our walking tour, the things that make Anywhere High School a safe place:

- Principal, vice-principals greet students, look for dress code and other violations

- Access restricted to front doors; other doors locked
- Teachers out in hallways during passing periods
- Security guard reminds some students to slow down in hallway
- Late student takes responsibility to report to attendance office for pass
- English teacher is engaging students; tolerances acceptable
- Lunchroom monitors circulate, talk to students, issue some reminders to be quiet

Now, let's look at the circumstances that aren't so safe:

- Lockers covered with graffiti, rust
- Teachers remain in their classrooms during passing periods
- Students shove one another through cramped doorways, run in hallway
- Security guard remains in his favorite corner instead of circulating
- Student opens side door and leaves it ajar
- Student yells at attendance clerk; no consequence for yelling
- Math teacher out of touch with class; tolerances too high
- No orderly passing routine to lunchroom
- Lunchroom monitors arrive after students; tolerances too high regarding yelling, behavior
- Monitors congregate in one area and chat
- Students don't dispose of lunch trash, trays after eating
- Intercom system, water fountain need repairs
- Hallways need repainting

You can see by the two lists that making and keeping a school safe means successfully combining factors involving the relationships between the members of the school community, including establishment and enforcement of tolerances, and ongoing stewardship of the physical plant that is the school building.

School safety is a complex issue. Sometimes people try to simplify it. They want to install a metal detector, hire a security guard, or pass a zero-tolerance weapons policy. They believe these actions will automatically make their schools safer.

Unfortunately, it's just not that easy. Violence in society stems from so many factors that pinpointing a single safety solution is not only simplistic, it's foolhardy. Different schools will require a combination of different strategies to keep violence at bay, but all can benefit from an administration that works to foster relationships with students and to create a sense of responsibility to one another among all who are part of the school community. We've talked about these ideas in earlier chapters of this book.

In this chapter, we'll look at some nuts-and-bolts techniques for keeping schools safe, including how to develop a safety plan for your school, and how to reach outside your building – to families and the community – to forge partnerships that can make a difference for your students.

◆ Safety and Learning

Feeling safe, like having air to breathe and food to eat, is a fundamental human need. If those needs are not met, our bodies will not have the physical fortification they require to accomplish other tasks. Take something as simple as hunger, for example. Have you ever tried to finish up paperwork or do another task when you're very hungry? It can be extremely difficult to concentrate and ignore those hunger pangs!

Now think about feeling safe. Think about the teenager who attends a large high school in a part of town known for its high crime rate. It's probably going to be pretty hard for that student to think about his English paper when he's just been threatened with "Better watch your back, Waterboy. I'm comin' after you" by the school's most notorious gang member.

So whatever you as a teacher or administrator can do to remove safety issues as impediments to learning, you must do. Use the information in this chapter as a guideline for measuring what tasks await your school as you strive for a safer environment. And remember: The work continues every day because, unfortunately, there are always new safety challenges.

◆ Characteristics of a Safe School

Take a look at the environment in your school. Does it feel safe? Review the following U.S. Department of Education list of risk factors that make a school unsafe, then review the following characteristics of a safe school. Which list best describes your school?

An unsafe school has:
- Poor design and use of space
- Overcrowding
- Lack of caring but firm disciplinary procedures
- Insensitivity and poor accommodation to multicultural factors
- Student alienation

- Rejection of at-risk students by teachers and peers
- Anger and resentment at school routines and demands for conformity
- Poor supervision

A safe school:
- Has an environment that is orderly and purposeful
- Is free from threats of physical or psychological harm
- Displays sensitivity and respect for all
- Demonstrates clear behavioral expectations and consistent disciplinary policies
- Recognizes positive behaviors
- Has proactive security measures and established response plans
- Is clean, regularly maintained, and has an attractive appearance
- Has a strong sense of community among students, staff, and families

In addition to these qualities, here are some additional safe-school qualities[1] to consider:

▶**Emphasize positive relationships among staff and students:** Effective schools make sure that opportunities exist for adults to spend quality, personal time with youth. Effective schools also encourage students to develop solid relationships with each other and to help one another.

▶**Discuss safety issues openly:** Teach youngsters about the dangers of firearms, and discuss strategies they can use to deal with their feelings and express them appropriately. Schools also should teach youth that they are responsible for their actions and they will be held responsible for the choices they make.

▶ **Encourage staff to discuss safety issues, including comparing notes on students who may have the potential for causing harm:** If the student in your fourth-period art class seems preoccupied with death in her artwork, ask the English teacher if the student's work in that class echoes the same themes. If so, maybe there's a reason to talk with the student and her family or ask the school counselor to meet with the student.

▶ **Develop a confidential process for students to report potential safety threats:** Youngsters usually are the first to know if a peer is contemplating violence. Schools need a process so students can report a threat or plan to hurt students or teachers. Some districts have student telephone "hotlines" or computer e-mail where students can provide information confidentially or anonymously. Another method might be for all students to fill out an anonymous form each week answering some simple questions: "Did you feel safe in school this week? If not, why?" and "Are there any safety issues you're concerned about in the coming week?"

▶ **Teach students that they are not betraying a classmate if they provide information about a fellow student:** Rather, this is a way to help a peer, and keep all students safe. Encourage students to confide in a caring adult if they believe their school could be vulnerable to a violent act. And remember that sometimes students will "report" their concerns about a peer by talking to another student about that peer when a teacher is within earshot. Keep your ears open for this kind of "reporting."

▶ **Help students feel safe about expressing their feelings:** Students should feel comfortable telling teachers and school staff about their feelings, needs, and fears. Without a group of caring adults, youngsters may feel isolated and rejected and may choose acting-out behaviors.

▶ **Promote good citizenship and character:** Schools have an academic mission, but they also must help students become good citizens by supporting the civic values set forth in the Constitution and Bill of Rights. In addition, schools should reinforce the shared values of their communities: honesty, kindness, responsibility, and respect for others.

▶ **Identify threats to safety and find solutions:** Teachers and school staff should be continuously aware of persons or situations that pose a threat to safety, and effective methods need to be developed to remove those threats. Consider your school's truancy, dropout, and on-campus crime rates as factors that influence how safe your building is. Provide training in warning signs so the entire school community – teachers, students, parents, support staff – can identify dangerous situations and students in trouble and find a way to help.

▶ **Simplify staff requests for urgent assistance:** Make sure your action plan is flexible enough to respond quickly when circumstances warrant.

At the core of a safe and effective school is a solid academic program where principals, teachers, students, and parents agree on the goals, methods, and content of curriculum and support the principles of publicly recognizing students who succeed. This promotes a sense of school pride and zealously protects school time for learning.

The principal has a vision for what an effective and safe school is and systematically works to bring that vision to life. He or she establishes strong instructional leadership that emphasizes basic skills and academic achievement. The principal makes clear, consistent, and fair decisions.

The principal hires highly motivated teachers with exceptional academic credentials who have good values, good social skills, and good judgment. The principal creates opportunities for ongoing staff education and encourages a climate of cooperation and achievement. The principal consistently enforces school rules, as well as a routine that discourages disorder and disruptions.

In a safe and effective school, teachers manage busy, vibrant classrooms where each student is valued and reinforced and where high expectations are nurtured. In these classrooms, teachers believe that all students can and will learn. These teachers energetically pursue parental involvement.

In a safe and effective school, students understand and follow classroom and school rules and have a sense of identity and pride in their school. They understand and agree that their first priority is to learn, and they make every effort to contribute to academic achievement by participating in classroom activities and completing homework assignments. Above all, they have learned to respect one another.

As you begin to assess your school's safety, you will undoubtedly discover that it already has many of the qualities we've discussed here. Nevertheless, you will want to make efforts to strengthen those qualities and formulate a plan to introduce missing qualities.

As we've discussed elsewhere in this book, adopting the Boys Town Education Model for use in your school may be a way to introduce some of those missing elements and make your school a safer, more effective place. The Model, with its flexible teaching methods, helps principals and teachers establish a routine that provides clear guidelines for students, so they know which behaviors will and will not be tolerated.

Social or life skills instruction is an important component of making schools safer. Many youth in school today have few skills in such basic interpersonal interaction (Walker, Colvin, & Ramsey, 1995). Because of that, the probability of negative peer and adult interactions is increased, along with an attendant increase in the potential for aggressive and violent acting out.

If you include life skills instruction in your curriculum, make every effort to ensure that the skills you teach not only help students in the school setting, but also are valid with peers.

You may find that life skills instruction pays off in more than just a better atmosphere in the classroom. Many teachers have found that when their students become proficient in social skills, there is more time in the classroom for academics because teachers don't have to spend as much time correcting students and dealing with acting-out behavior.

Remember that the Boys Town Education Model cannot replace strong, effective teachers, administrators, or curriculum. The Model is *not* a substitute for good instructional practices.

◆ Safety Plans for Teachers and Buildings

In light of shootings and other violence in American school buildings, many principals are developing action plans that serve two purposes – first and foremost, preventing violence, and second, providing structure for managing a violent episode, should one occur.

As you begin to think about developing a plan for your school, consider the following points developed by Dr. Ken C. Strong (Strong, 1996):

- Violence can happen at any school.

- No two violent events can be handled the same way.

- Review your action plan annually.

- Make sure your plan contains these elements: a clear chain of command, the ability to communicate both within the building and outside to contact law enforcement and rescue personnel, and knowledge of what roles those at the school building will play and what roles district officials will play.

Strong also identified the following four sets of steps in preparing schools to handle a crisis:

◆ Crisis Preparedness I

- Learn to read early and imminent warning signs in youngsters. These signs are discussed later in this chapter.

- Develop a school plan or adopt your district's action plan for use in your building. Use the information in these checklists to help you develop components of the plan. Review the plan with staff and students to ensure that everyone knows what to do.

- The plan should have provisions for keeping everyone safe both inside and outside the school building.

- If your building has a school nurse, consider what direct-care roles he or she might play in a crisis and which staff members have training or could be trained to assist the nurse.

- Use the school intercom for emergency announcements and instructions during a crisis. Investigate how classrooms, the library, gymnasium, and other locations will communicate with the office if your building does not have a two-way communications system.

- Make sure your local police and fire departments have blueprints of your school building.

- Assign each staff member a role to assume during a crisis, including protecting students, communications, first aid, evacuation, etc. Whenever possible, have a backup person for each responsibility in case the primary person is unable to fulfill his or her duties. Try to scatter responsibilities among staff throughout the building so people with different expertise will be available in different areas. Review crisis roles regularly so each person knows what to do. Make sure new staff members become familiar with your building plan and know what role they are to play.

- Teach students that their first duty in a crisis is to listen to adults and do exactly as they are told. Also review any other rules with students, including if they are to move to a certain area, dive under their desks, etc.

◆ Crisis Preparedness II

- Establish a clear chain of command.
- Prepare an emergency kit with medical supplies and other items that may be needed.
- Establish procedures for identifying the injured.
- Identify a command post.
- Be ready for the media. You may want to identify one person to handle all media inquiries.
- Develop plans for transportation, crowd control, student release, and evacuation.

◆ Crisis Management

- Execute the plan as practiced: take charge immediately, summon help, identify the injured, provide first aid and support to victims, verify absent students.
- Manage the media: establish a media command post, hold structured news conferences, be truthful, control access to students.
- Implement a transportation plan.
- Control the crowd.
- Provide information and support to family and friends.

◆ Crisis Resolution

- Give accurate information to teachers, students, parents.
- Visit injured in the hospital.
- Offer professional counseling to students, families, teachers, and staff.

- Reopen school as soon as possible.
- Give students time to work through the crisis.
- Have an open house for students and their families.
- If a death has occurred, hold a memorial service if appropriate, but not if the death is a suicide.

◆ Safety in School Buildings

We've looked at a variety of measures for increasing safety in schools, most involving procedures you can develop. The following suggestions from the U.S. Department of Education's "Early Warning, Timely Response" relate to keeping the physical structure of your school safe:

- Supervise access to the building and grounds.
- Reduce class size and school size.
- Adjust class schedules to minimize the amount of time students spend in hallways or in potentially dangerous locations. Consider modifying traffic flow patterns to limit the potential for altercations.
- Conduct a building safety audit with school security personnel or law enforcement officials.
- Close school campuses during lunch periods.
- Adopt a school policy on uniforms.
- Arrange supervision at critical times, such as in hallways between classes. Have a plan to deploy supervisory staff to areas where incidents are likely to occur.

- Prohibit students from congregating in areas where they are likely to break rules or use intimidating or aggressive behaviors.
- Have adults visibly present throughout the school building. This includes encouraging parents to visit the school.
- Stagger dismissal times and lunch periods.
- Monitor the surrounding school grounds, including landscaping, parking lots, and bus stops.
- Coordinate with local police to ensure that there are safe routes to and from school.
- Identify safe areas in the school where students and staff should go in the event of a crisis.

As you develop your crisis plan and make other efforts to improve safety at your school, keep in mind what impact certain components of the plan may have on your school.

For example, some schools have posted security guards in their buildings and installed metal detectors. Measures like these can make adults feel safer, but they may actually create more anxiety for some students. You will need to balance the need for security at your school with the daily impact those security measures could have on your students and staff.

Another example of an anti-violence measure that many schools have adopted is the zero-tolerance policy. But such policies, which impose strict, high-profile consequences for using violence, can backfire.

Consider, for example, the case of a sixth-grader in South Carolina who brought a steak knife in her lunch box to cut chicken. She asked her teacher if she could use the knife, but never got to because police were called and the girl was taken away in a cruiser. She was suspended and threatened with expulsion (Skiba, 1998).

Or, there was the case of the California third-grader who was expelled after he got into a scuffle with another boy on the playground during a tetherball game. The principal said the expulsion was her only choice under the district's zero-tolerance policy because the boy had a previous violation: He had been suspended for five days for twisting the finger of a girl who he said was "saying bad things in line" (Skiba, 1998).

Zero-tolerance policies attempt to control violence or other problems, such as drug use, by maximizing the punishment for even small infractions in order to send out a message that these behaviors will not be tolerated.

But as these examples show, a student can receive the maximum punishment for even a minimal violation. That can send the wrong message to a student.

The girl with the steak knife, for example, may decide that she should "go for broke" and really cause havoc at school. After all, she tried to do the right thing by asking her teacher if she could use the knife to cut the chicken in her lunch, but instead was whisked away in a police cruiser and then suspended.

She's already gotten nearly the maximum punishment for an unintentional infraction. The next time she's tempted to get in trouble, she might think: "I might as well go ahead and go for it. That trip in the police cruiser was kind of cool, and I got to stay home for a few days and watch TV. It really wasn't that bad."

A survey of a computer database of newspaper stories related to student suspensions and expulsions found that between May 1 and July 1, 1998, there were a total of 216 stories of separate incidents of suspensions and expulsions. They ranged from youth writing notes that said, "Kill, kill, kill," to a child being suspended for opening up a school computer with a pen-knife (Donohue, Schiraldi, & Ziedenberg, 1998).

Donohue, Schiraldi, and Ziedenberg reported that the 216 stories represented only a sampling of American newspapers, so more suspensions and expulsions actually could have occurred in response to zero-tolerance policies.

Remember that decisions you make can have unintended effects on your students, so choose the components of your crisis plan with care. You don't want to end up with more issues to deal with than you already have.

◆ Intervention

Intervening in the life of a student is never easy. However, it may be a life-saving action. The relationships you build with students will give you insight into their behaviors and hopefully provide advance warning if a crisis is imminent. That way, you will be able to intervene and possibly prevent a violent episode in your school.

There are a variety of ways to intervene. Many are very effective. However, some methods make matters worse, such as arguing with an angry teenager. Getting into an argument with a youth only escalates a situation that's already volatile.

Keep in mind that some teenagers may view an intervention as a challenge, especially if the intervention is done in front of their friends. If you have students like this – who would turn a helping hand into a power struggle – try talking to them privately. By choosing the right time, place, and skill to work on, you will do fewer interventions to stop negative behavior.

You also can use Preventive Prompts to remind youngsters what they should be doing as a way to point them in the right direction behaviorally. For more information about the use of prompts, see Chapter 9 on Proactive Teaching.

Before you begin an intervention process to stop a behavior, you may need to assess that behavior to determine why the youngster is acting the way he or she is acting.

▶ What is the "payoff" to the student?
What is the youngster receiving in exchange for the behavior he or she is undertaking? Do people usually let Randy get his way when he starts bullying them? That means he's learned that he just has to act big and tough when he wants to throw his weight around. You'll want to talk with him about more appropriate ways to get what he wants.

▶ See if you can determine what sparks the behavior.
What usually happens just before the behavior occurs? Do you see a pattern? Does Emily usually lose her temper when somebody is teasing her? Then your intervention will include a discussion with Emily about how she can control her temper when she's being teased.

▶ Look at your own behavior.
Make sure you're not doing anything to fan the flames of bad behavior, such as arguing with students, bullying them, or subjecting them to a heavy dose of sarcasm.

Intervention may be done with individual students or groups of students. Walker, Colvin, and Ramsey (1995) define interventions with groups of students as *universal interventions.* These may include such efforts as life skills training for all students in regular classrooms or implementing a schoolwide discipline plan. You may want to consult other Boys Town Press publications as you develop intervention programs in your building, including the Life Skills Curriculum (with accompanying lesson plans and activities), a companion to this book, and *Teaching Social Skills to Youth.*

Interventions with individual students are *selected interventions.* Examples of selected interventions include individual counseling, interventions described earlier in this book, and specialized programs for aggressive students.

Universal interventions tend to be prevention oriented and usually work best for students who are beginning to dabble in antisocial behavior or are at risk for involvement in those kinds of behaviors. Selected interventions often are used with youngsters for whom other behavior-changing efforts have been unsuccessful.

Young people's behaviors may signal how deeply they're involved in potentially violent activities, giving you some information about the type of intervention to use. Dwyer, Osher, and Warger (1998) identified the following Early Warning Signs and Imminent Warning Signs that may help stave off aggressive or violent actions. The authors urge caution, however, that the signs not be misinterpreted and that those who use the signs to interpret students' behavior keep these principles in mind:

◆ Principles for Identifying the Early Warning Signs of School Violence

▶ **Do no harm:** Make sure that you use the warning signs as a way to help students, not as a vehicle for excluding, punishing, or stereotyping them. If you suspect that a student has a particular disabling condition or needs counseling or other assistance, contact the proper agencies or authorities. Remember that all referrals to outside agencies must be confidential and you must have parental consent, except in the case of suspected abuse or neglect.

▶ **Understand violence and aggression within a context:** Violent and aggressive behaviors as an expression of emotion may be rooted in a variety of factors that exist within the school, the home, or the community. For young people who are at risk for aggression and violence, certain environments or situations may set off violent reactions. Use your relationships with students to help you learn what their "triggers" are and work with them to develop anti-aggressive responses to the triggers.

▶ **Avoid stereotypes:** Don't let factors like race, socio-economic status, physical appearance, or cognitive or academic ability become false cues that prompt action against a youth. Such stereotypes are unfair and can harm youth, especially when their school community acts on them.

▶ **View warning signs within a developmental context:** Students at different levels of development have different social and emotional capabilities. Elementary, middle, and high school students express their needs differently.

▶ **Multiple warning signs are typical:** Research confirms that most youth who are troubled and at risk for aggression exhibit more than one warning sign, repeatedly and with increasing intensity over time. Because of this, it is important not to overreact to single signs, words, or actions.

◆ Early Warning Signs

It is not always possible to predict violent behavior. However, a good rule of thumb is to assume that these warning signs, especially when they are presented in combination, indicate you should take a closer look at the student to see if intervention is warranted. Research shows that most youth who become violent toward themselves or others feel rejected or psychologically victimized. In most cases, students who exhibit aggressive behavior early in life will, without support, progress toward severe aggression or violence. However, research also shows that when young people have a positive, meaningful connection to an adult, whether at home, in school, or in the community, the potential for violence is significantly reduced. The early warning signs (Dwyer, Osher, & Warger, 1998) include:

▶ **Social withdrawal:** Gradual and eventually complete withdrawal from social contacts can be an important indicator of a troubled youth. The withdrawal can stem from depression, rejection, persecution, unworthiness, and lack of confidence.

▶ **Excessive feelings of isolation:** Many students who are isolated and appear friendless are not violent. In fact, these feelings may be part and parcel of other problems they have that hinder sociability. However, research also has shown that in some cases, feelings of isolation are associated with youngsters who behave aggressively and violently.

▶ **Excessive feelings of rejection:** Many young people experience rejection, particularly during their teen years. How they respond to that rejection depends in large part on their backgrounds. Without support, they may use violent behavior as an outlet for their feelings of rejection.

▶ **Being a victim of violence:** Students who are victims of violence, including physical or sexual abuse, may be at risk of becoming violent toward themselves or others.

▶ **Feelings of persecution:** The youth who continually feels picked on, teased, bullied, or humiliated – at home or at school – may withdraw. Without support, he or she may react violently to those feelings of being persecuted.

▶ **Marginal academic interest, performance:** A student who is not achieving in school may feel frustrated, unworthy, and denigrated and may display aggressive behaviors. It's important to put the low achievement in perspective. Is this new or chronic behavior? What may be causing the lack of academic success? Is the environment in your classrooms so unsafe that concentration and learning is next to impossible? Do kids feel safer in the office than in your classrooms?

▶ **Expressing violence in writings, drawings:** Youth often express their thoughts, feelings, desires, and intentions in their drawings, poetry, and stories. Many students produce works with violent themes, but often it is not a threat that they will become violent. However, excessively violent drawings and writings that are directed at specific individuals, such as a parent, teacher, or peer, may signal emotional problems and the potential for violence if the works appear consistently over time. Because there is a real danger in misdiagnosing such a sign, consult a school psychologist, counselor, or other mental health professional to assist you.

▶ **Uncontrolled anger:** A student who expresses anger frequently and intensely in response to minor irritants may signal potential violent behavior toward self or others.

▶ **Patterns of impulsive and chronic hitting, intimidating, and bullying**

behaviors: Youth often shove each other and exhibit mild forms of aggression. However, some mildly aggressive behaviors such as constant hitting and bullying that occur in early childhood, if left unattended, might escalate later into more serious behaviors.

▶ **History of discipline problems:** Chronic behavior and disciplinary problems, both in school and at home, may suggest that emotional needs are not being met. These unmet needs may result in acting out and aggressive behaviors. These problems may set the stage for the youth to violate rules, defy authority, disengage from school, and engage in aggressive behaviors with other youth and adults.

▶ **History of violent and aggressive behavior:** Without support and counseling, a youth with a history of aggressive or violent behavior is likely to repeat those behaviors. Aggressive and violent acts may be directed toward others, be expressed in cruelty to animals, or include fire-setting. Students who show an early pattern of antisocial behavior in a variety of settings are at risk for future aggressive and antisocial behavior. Similarly, students who engage in overt behaviors like bullying and covert behaviors like stealing, vandalism, lying, and fire-setting are at risk for more serious behavior. Research shows that the younger students are when they begin using aggressive behavior, the more likely it will continue as they grow older.

▶ **Intolerance and prejudicial attitudes:** An intense prejudice toward others, based on racial, ethnic, religious, sexual orientation, or other differences may lead to violent assaults against those who are thought to be different. Membership in hate groups or the willingness to victimize individuals with disabilities or health problems also should be considered as early warning signs.

▶ **Drug and alcohol use:** Using drugs and alcohol reduces self-control and exposes youth to violence, either as perpetrators, victims, or both.

▶ **Gang affiliation:** Students who are influenced by gangs or join them tend to support gang's antisocial values such as extortion, intimidation, and violent acts.

▶ **Possession and use of firearms:** Youth who inappropriately possess or have access to firearms can have an increased risk for violence and a higher probability of becoming victims. Families should restrict, monitor, and supervise their youngsters' access to weapons, and young people with a history of aggressiveness, impulsiveness, or other emotional problems should have no access to firearms.

▶ **Serious threats of violence:** Idle threats can be a common response to frustration, but one of the most reliable indicators that a youth is likely to commit a dangerous act is a detailed and specific threat to use violence. In several recent school shootings, threats were uttered prior to the violent acts being completed. Steps must be taken to understand the nature of these threats and to prevent them from being carried out.

◆ Imminent Warning Signs

Unlike early warning signs, imminent warning signs indicate that a student is very close to acting in a way that could hurt himself or herself or others. Imminent warning signs require an immediate response.

No single warning sign can predict that a dangerous act will occur. Instead, imminent warning signs usually come as a sequence of overt, serious, hostile behaviors directed at others. Usually, more than one person is aware of these signs, which may include:

- Serious physical fighting with peers or family members
- Severe destruction of property
- Severe rage for seemingly minor reasons
- Detailed threats of lethal violence
- Possession and/or use of firearms and other weapons
- Other self-injurious behaviors or threats of suicide

◆ Resiliency

It is important to remember the concept of resiliency as you work to develop relationships with your students.

Researchers from a variety of disciplines have used the term *resilience* to describe the phenomenon where youth attain good outcomes even though they were at risk to fail. They may come from families torn by abuse or alcoholism, for example, or perhaps lost a parent to violence early in life.

These students seem to exemplify the adage, "When the going gets tough, the tough get going." In simple terms, resilience is the ability to bounce back when bad things happen. No matter what kind of obstacles life throws in their way, resilient students not only overcome them, but triumph.

Garmezy (1985) identified three categories of protective factors that may contribute to resiliency. They are the child's personality, a sup-

portive family, and an external support system that encourages and reinforces his or her coping efforts.

Schools can help resilient students by becoming part of that external support system. Teachers, school staff, administrators, and older peers can serve as mentors to these students, encouraging them to hone their academic and social skills and helping them become involved in school activities.

◆ Impact on Violence in Society

Just as schools can nurture resiliency in some students and help them resist falling into antisocial or violent behavior patterns, schools also can build relationships with the families and communities they serve and use those relationships to deter violence (Walker, Colvin, & Ramsey, 1995).

For example, schools can develop strong communication with families that foster cooperation and mutual respect, creating a foundation for home-school partnerships that encourage achievement. In addition, schools may become centers for neighborhood or community activities, helping to unify the area against crime and gang activity. Sociological research indicates that a community or neighborhood's level of social disorganization is a strong predictor of gang activity, delinquency, and crime victimization (Sampson, 1992). Social disorganization is the absence of a sense of neighborhood cohesion – conflicting values, social isolation, and a lack of neighborhood support networks. This disorganization directly relates to a neighborhood's ability to control delinquency and crime.

More information on school-community partnerships is discussed in the following sections.

◆ Building Partnerships with Families

The most successful school-family partnerships reach out to all families, particularly those who are isolated or inactive, in an effort to get them more involved in school life. Students whose families are actively involved in their school lives are more likely to get better grades and less likely to be drawn to delinquent or criminal behaviors.

Sometimes, it's difficult to get families involved. Language barriers, racial differences, and poor education may mean families don't understand the importance of being involved in their children's schools. Work schedules may prevent them from attending teacher conferences and school events.

The 1991 Council for Exceptional Children (CEC) Conference in Atlanta established that, in the 1990s, we can expect to see more of the following: working mothers, latchkey children, cultural and economic diversity, children in poverty, homeless families, and children in extended day care. Schools are increasingly charged with the responsibility of providing extended use of their facilities to serve children and their families, particularly those at risk.

Often, parents have had negative relationships with schools when they were students. Because of this, parents come to their children's schools with preconceived negative expectations.

Meanwhile, teachers can develop low expectations of parents, which creates another obstacle to helping the student. The upshot of all this negative feeling is unproductive blame-trading.

When faced with overwhelming problems, such as those outlined at the CEC Conference, parents are little concerned with trying to work with teachers. On the other hand, teachers are pressured to involve parents without adequate resources or time to do so. Few have had the supplemental education to work with parents, and it is not part of their contractual obligation (Betty Phillips Center for Parenthood Education, 1992).

Children spend six to ten hours a day in school and/or extended care programming. Therefore, schools have become responsible for teaching not only academics, but addressing social and emotional issues as well. Without parental support, schools will most likely fail in their efforts to teach children skills they can generalize.

When teachers develop positive relationships with their students' parents, they give their students the best opportunity to get the best possible education. In order to achieve that goal, teachers must find methods to develop rapport and build a team relationship with families and to share information about the school program with families.

Sometimes, schools take a narrow approach to making those connections with parents. The district might hold a parent workshop or set up a homework hotline (Burch & Palanki, 1994). But a better approach is to offer more options because the more opportunities families have to get involved, the more likely they are to get involved. Administrators can help their teachers with this effort by ensuring that adequate resources are available for work with parents and that teachers are recognized and reinforced for positive interactions with parents (Smallwood, Hawryluk, & Pierson, 1990).

Here are some suggestions for involving families in the life of your school:

▶ **Get to know the families of your students.** Make telephone calls to talk with them about a student's progress. Don't just call when there's bad news to report; find a positive accomplishment to laud. Send a note home offering congratulations for a success the student had. Ask parents to sign homework assignments. When you have to make a call about a concern with a student, use the "no fault" approach – emphasize how you and the parents can work together to increase the student's success. Note any attempts the student has made to improve his or her situation, and end the telephone conversation on a positive note.

▶ **Take advantage of technology to ease communication.** Use voice mail, electronic mail, and other forms of messaging to supplement telephone calls and in-person meetings. These types of communication can be helpful to keep connected with busy parents, but make sure these aren't your only points of contact with them.

▶ **Try to get families into the school building regularly.** Offer incentives such as a simple pizza dinner or a series of short evening workshops on making youngsters better students. Several states, including Kentucky and California, are experimenting with family resource centers that are attached to school districts. These centers offer support, assistance, and training to parents and also allow parents to deal with their children's school-related problems in a nonjudgmental atmosphere. The centers have the potential to build effective school-family teams.

▶ **When families visit school, make them feel comfortable.** Get an interpreter if you don't speak the family's language and they don't speak English. Offer a cup of coffee or a snack, and praise the child's accomplishments. Try to understand and respect the family's values. All these efforts will help you establish a relationship with the family, which can improve the child's chances for success.

▶ **Recruit parent volunteers to help with classroom projects.** Identify the volunteers through a postcard survey you conduct at the beginning of the year that lists parents' talents and times they are available to help. Set up a room in your school for volunteers and store parent resource materials there. Establish a "telephone tree" among your families to keep them informed about classroom activities (Epstein, Coates, Salinas, Sanders, & Simon, 1997).

▶ **Inform parents if you are experiencing antisocial or aggressive behavior patterns in a student or see behaviors that could be classified as early or imminent warning signs.** Work with the family to develop a school-home intervention plan.

▶ **Keep families updated on your school safety plan.** Provide them with a telephone number they can call in the event of a crisis. Outline what the dismissal procedure will be in an emergency situation, and provide them with other necessary information.

▶ **Give parents information about what they can do at home to help students with homework assignments.** Develop a regular schedule of homework assignments that require students to interact with parents or other family members. Get families involved in setting student goals each year (Epstein, Coates, Salinas, Sanders, & Simon, 1997).

▶ Include parents in making decisions that affect students' school life. Actively recruit PTA/PTO officers and members. Appoint parents to curriculum, safety, personnel, and other school committees (Epstein, Coates, Salinas, Sanders, & Simon, 1997).

Parent-Teacher Conferences

The productive relationships that teachers build with parents provide students with greater consistency in the two most important environments in their lives. When there's open communication and a good working relationship between home and school, kids have more opportunities to learn and grow. Stephens and Wolf (1980) recommend a four-step sequence for parent-teacher conferences to maximize the outcome of the meeting.

▶ **The first step is building rapport with the parents.** Before you get down to business, spend a few moments engaging in small talk to break the ice and set the stage for a conversation among adult equals. As you begin the meeting, say something positive about the student. That gets the conference off to a positive start.

▶ **Second, obtain pertinent information from the parents.** Questions such as "What has Alex told you about my class?", should open the door for the parents to share information or concerns. Be willing to take some time to discuss the parents' goals for their child throughout the conference.

▶ **Third, provide specific information about what the child is doing in school and share samples of his or her work.** It is important to share the student's strengths even within an area that requires further development.

▶ **Fourth, summarize what was said and discuss any follow-up activities.** Parents should also leave the conference with a copy of everything that was discussed.

Your behavior during the conference will greatly affect its outcome. Keep the following considerations in mind as you meet with parents:

- It usually is best to assume that the parents know the most about the child and his or her needs.

- Always consider the parents' perspective when discussing what is best for the child.

- If you make a suggestion, start with something the parents can do successfully, and do not be defensive or intimidated if they disagree with you. Instead, ask for alternatives and be willing to compromise, but also be willing to take a youth advocacy stance on discipline and child protection issues.

- Most importantly, speak in plain and jargon-free language to avoid the appearance of being the "teacher-expert." This effort will help parents who may be intimidated by a teacher's educational background or parents who struggled when they were in school.

School-Home Notes, Newsletters, and More

Report cards are sent home too infrequently for parents to have an accurate picture of how their children fare daily at school. More frequent contact is needed to keep parents informed and to prevent small problems from mushrooming. Written contacts, such as a simple "happy gram" or a weekly newsletter, can fill the gaps between report cards or student-teacher conferences.

Newsletters that go home regularly are beneficial because they inform parents about everything from curriculum and class activities to upcoming school events and the lunch menu. Monthly calendars perform some of the same roles. And parent handbooks can be an ongoing resource for families throughout the school year.

Some teachers use the school/home note to communicate with parents. These notes are useful when daily contact is warranted due to a student's ongoing behavioral or academic problems. The note is a two-way communication device that serves as a daily "report card" on the student's activities. The frequency of feedback that both you and the parents receive is maximized and issues can be dealt with quickly, which enhances your overall effectiveness.

The school note functions best as part of a "contract" contingency, with rewards for school behavior being given at home based on classroom task completion or other predetermined criteria.

Communication between parents and school staff is critical if a school note program is to succeed. Don't start a program without parental involvement or consent, or all may be for naught. In fact, a teacher who barrels ahead with a school note without consulting a student's parents may be seen as punitive.

When teachers and parents meet to determine the goal of a school note, it is important to keep the focus narrow and to concentrate on one to three behaviors at a time. The teacher should know what reinforcers and consequences are associated with the note. The teacher is then responsible for filling out the note contingently and consistently, always noting more positive behaviors than negative behaviors. Any design of school note may be used, as long as it is easy to read, specific, and quick to fill out.

Roadblocks to Parental Involvement

Teachers may have the best intentions to help children succeed in school and in fact may have put forth a great deal of effort to involve parents and keep them informed. But sometimes those efforts fail because of family problems over which teachers have no control. Some of those problems are detailed here:

▶ **Apathy:** When it appears that parents have given up on their children and make statements to that regard, it is important to say and do things that model hopefulness. The teacher also can make an impact by reinforcing any enthusiasm or interest and by asking questions or making comments that may bring out positive responses.

▶ **Unreliable parents:** The best approach with parents who seem to be unreliable is to use preventive and educational methods. That is, let parents know what you need and when and why you need it. Before you label a parent as unreliable, however, make an effort to see if there is an underlying reason. For example, a parent who relies on public transportation may have trouble attending school events in the evenings, as might a parent who's working more than one job to make ends meet. Teachers must be open to alternative solutions in these cases, such as meeting at the family's home or having a telephone meeting. Keep in mind that some parents who have had negative school experiences may not feel welcome or may feel intimidated. When individuals feel they have nothing to contribute, it is difficult for them to be motivated. It is important to be welcoming and reinforcing and offer parents meaningful roles with which they will feel comfortable.

▶ **Hostile and uncooperative parents:** When faced with an angry parent, it is imperative to remain calm and professional. Try to use a combination of problem-solving and empathy to bring the parent around, but remember that you may have to simply end the meeting and have a school administrator mediate all subsequent meetings. Always review your own behavior to make sure you're not doing something or saying something to alienate others. Seek feedback from colleagues and others on whether you present a professional image. Telling parents that their input is valuable is an important step to take. If you find yourself in a discussion with an intoxicated parent, do not try to reason with him or her, but end the conversation tactfully and as quickly as possible. Do not get into a situation where you could be injured. Ask for administrative assistance.

▶ **Severe personal problems of parents:** This is a difficult area to change, due to the lack of control that teachers have over parents' behavior. Resist the temptation to act as a counselor, except to refer parents to a school social worker who may be able to tell them about agencies that are able to provide services.

▶ **Abusive and neglectful parents:** When discovered, abuse and neglect must be reported to the proper authorities and agencies. To ensure that the school is a safe environment for children, policies and procedures should be followed to the letter.

The bottom line is that kids do better in school when their parents and teachers work together, but both parents and teachers are faced with limited time and resources. If we are to improve the quality of education for children in the 21st century, we must overcome some of the seemingly insurmountable barriers. We must join hands for our kids, as in the African proverb, "It takes a village to raise a child."

◆ Building Partnerships with the Community

Schools are microcosms of society. So problems like violence that embattle our streets are more than likely to flare up in our classrooms, too.

When schools join forces with their communities to reduce violence, many opportunities arise for partnership and problem-solving to improve the lives of students. The best school-community programs feature:

▶ **An after-school component:** Most juvenile offenses occur after school. Data from the FBI's National Incident-Based Reporting System show that one in five violent crimes committed by juveniles occur in the four hours following the end of the school day (between 2-6 p.m.) These programs can offer a voluntary safety net that can catch many at-risk students and also provide enriching experiences and programs.[2]

One successful school-community program, the Baltimore Police Athletic League (PAL), operates during those critical hours. PAL programs are run from 2-10 p.m. with a focus on these four components: character development, home assistance and academic achievement, arts and cultural activities, and physical activities.

Full-service, or "Beacon" schools, which operate in New York, offer another juvenile crime prevention alternative. These schools remain open until about 8 p.m., offering recre-

▶ 133

ational, educational, and counseling activities to their students until working parents can pick up their youngsters.

▶ **A broad definition of community:** You can define community as broadly as you want, involving as many agencies as is viable to address needs in your area. In California's San Diego County, for example, a large collaboration of organizations and agencies has come together to keep schools safe and effective. The collaboration was born to battle issues including high unemployment and an increase in juvenile violence and crime.

Joining efforts are San Diego community-based organizations, the PTA, and leaders from education, health care, social services, the faith community, law enforcement, juvenile court, universities, and 43 school districts. Efforts developed include a prevention and early intervention program that targets juvenile offenders and gang members, anti-drug and anti-violence programs in schools, health services initiatives, and after-school activities for middle schoolers.

Another way to involve a broad spectrum of the community is to form a school safety committee, which includes not only teachers, staff, and students, but parents and community representatives such as police officers, firefighters, juvenile justice officials, business people, and lawmakers. Having nonschool representatives on your school committees broadens the perspective and expertise available to your district.

▶ **Lending a hand:** Partnerships can help community groups as well as your school. Get students involved in community activities such as recycling, offering services to senior citizens, Special Olympics, etc. (Epstein, Coates, Salinas, Sanders, & Simon, 1997).

[1]Source: "Early Warning, Timely Response: A Guide to Safe Schools," August 1998. "Early Warning, Timely Response" was produced by the Center for Effective Collaboration and Practice of the American Institutes for Research in collaboration with the National Association of School Psychologists, under a cooperative agreement with the U.S. Department of Education, Office of Special Education and Rehabilitative Services, Office of Special Education Programs.

[2]Sickmund, Melissa; Snyder, Howard N., and Poe-Yamagara, Eileen, (1997). *Juvenile Offenders and Victims: 1997 Update on Violence.* Washington, DC: Office of Juvenile Justice and Delinquency Prevention., as reported in *School House Hype: School Shootings and the Real Risks Kids Face in America* (Elizabeth Donohue, Vincent Schiraldi, and Jason Ziedenberg, Justice Policy Institute, July 1998).

Chapter Summary

Anywhere High School
What's safe
What's unsafe

Safety and Learning

Characteristics of a Safe School

**Safety Plans for Teachers
and Buildings**

Crisis Preparedness I and II

Crisis Management

Crisis Resolution

Safety in School Buildings

Intervention

**Early Warning Signs of
School Violence**

Imminent Warning Signs

Resiliency

Impact on Violence in Society

**Building Partnerships
with Families**
Parent-Teacher Conferences
School-Home Notes
Newsletters
Roadblocks

**Building Partnerships with
the Community**

References

Astor, R. (1998). Moral reasoning about school violence: Informational assumptions about harm within school subcontexts. **Educational Psychologist, 33**(4), 207-221.

Betty Phillips Center for Parenthood Education (1992). **Parent involvement report, 2**(1). Nashville, TN: Peabody College, Vanderbilt University.

Burch, P., & Palanki, A. (1994) Parent-teacher action research: Supporting families through family-school-community partnerships. **Journal of Emotional and Behavioral Problems, 2**(4).

Dodge, K.A. (1991). The structure and function of reactive and proactive aggression. In D.J. Pepler & K.H. Rubin (Eds.), **The development and treatment of childhood aggression** (pp. 201-218). Hillsdale, NJ: Lawrence Erlbaum Associates Inc.

Donohue, E., Schiraldi, V., & Ziedenberg, J. (1998). Survey of Westlaw database. **School house hype: School shootings and the real risks kids face in America.** Washington, DC: Justice Policy Institute.

Dwyer, K., Osher, D., & Warger, C. (1998). **Early warning, timely response: A guide to safe schools.** Washington, DC: U.S. Department of Education.

Epstein, J.L., Coates, L., Salinas, K.C., Sanders, M.G., & Simon, B.S. (1997). **School, family, and community partnerships.** Thousand Oaks, CA: Cerwin Press.

Garmezy, N. (1985). Stress-resistant children: The search for protective factors. In J.E. Stevenson (Ed.), **Recent research in developmental psychopathology** (pp. 213-233). Elmsford, NY: Pergamon Press.

Halpern, D. (1996). **Thought and knowledge: An introduction to critical thinking.** Mahway. NJ: Lawrence Erlbaum Associates.

Henley, M., & Long, N. (1999). Teaching emotional intelligence to impulsive-aggressive youth. **Reclaiming Children and Youth, 7**(4), 224-229.

Hughes, J., & Hasbrouck, J. (1996). Television violence: Implications for violence prevention. **School Psychology Review, 25**(2), 134-151.

Lange, A.J., & Jakubowski, P. (1976). **Responsible assertive behavior: Cognitive/ behavioral procedures for trainers.** Champaign, IL: Research Press.

McKay, M., Davis, M., & Fanning, P. (1981). **Thoughts and feelings.** Oakland, CA: New Harbinger Publishers.

Miller, C.S. (1984). Building self-control. **Young Children,** 15-19.

Olweus, D. (1996). Bullying at school: Knowledge base and an effective intervention program. In C.F. Ferris & T. Grisso (Eds.), **Understanding aggressive behavior in children** (pp. 265-276). New York: The New York Academy of Sciences.

Patterson, G.R., Reid, J.B., & Dishion, T.J. (1992). **Antisocial boys: Vol. 4. A social interactional approach.** Eugene, OR: Castalia.

Peter, V.J. (1995). **Rules of clear thinking and the con artist.** Boys Town, NE: Father Flanagan's Boys' Home.

Sampson, R. (1992). Family management and child development: Insights from social disorganization theory. In J. McCord (Ed.), **Facts, frameworks, and forecasts: Advances in criminological theory, Vol 3.** (pp. 63-93). New Brunswick, NJ: Transaction Press.

Sickmund, M., Snyder, H.N., & Poe-Yamagara, E. (1997). **Juvenile offenders and victims:**

1997 update on violence. Washington, DC: Office of Juvenile Justice and Delinquency Prevention.

Skiba, R. (1998). **The dark side of zero tolerance: Can punishment lead to safe schools?** Presentation at IDEA Institute - Discipline Provisions: Positive Behavioral Supports and Beyond, Kansas City, MO.

Smallwood, D.L., Hawryluk, M.K., & Pierson, E. (1990). Promoting parent involvement in schools to serve at-risk students. In L.J. Kruger (Ed.), **Promoting success with at-risk students: Emerging perspectives and practical approaches.** New York: Haworth Press.

Sprague, J., & Walker, H. (1999). Early identification and intervention for antisocial and violent youth. Under review: **Exceptional Children.**

Stephens, T.M., & Wolf, J.S. (1980). **Effective skills in parent and teacher conferencing.** Columbus, OH: National Center for Educational Materials and Media for the Handicapped, Ohio State University.

Strong, K. (1996). **Building a foundation for safe schools.** Presentation to Mississippi Association of Psychologists in the Schools.

Walker, H. (1998). First steps to prevent antisocial behavior. **Teaching Exceptional Children, 30**(4), 16-19.

Walker, H., Colvin, G., & Ramsey, E. (1995). **Antisocial behavior in school: strategies and best practices.** Pacific Grove, CA: Brooks/Cole Publishing Co.

Index

The Boys Town Education Model
An Inclusive Approach to School Reform

As described in these pages, the Boys Town Education Model is adaptable to any school setting-public, private, or parochial. To assist individuals and organizations in applying the Model, Boys Town offers professional workshops, on-site training, and consultation services through its National Resource and Training Center (NRTC).

The NRTC provides research-based, outcome-oriented education programs for teachers, administrators, and parents. The programs reflect the Model's teaching philosophy of life skills, relationship-building, and self-empowerment, and together, represent a holistic approach to creating dynamic learning environments.

Youth-serving professionals interested in learning more about the Boys Town Model can take advantage of a variety of training workshops that include the following:

▶ **The Well-Managed Classroom** – This behavior management program emphasizes social skills instruction, empowering students to make better choices, be self-motivated, and become independent learners.

▶ **Reducing Aggression in Schools** – A "stop, think, then act" teaching model that encourages appropriate behavior in aggressive students is introduced, plus strategies for improving an educator's ability to handle confrontations.

▶ **Safe and Effective Secondary Schools** – This approach to safety in middle and secondary educational settings allows educators to create positive learning environments by developing curricula that include self-management, self-control, and relationship-building strategies.

▶ **The Well-Managed Classroom for Catholic Schools** – Specifically developed for Catholic school educators, this workshop introduces a proactive approach to developing curriculums that combine Catholic principles with the new three R's: respect, responsibility, and relationships.

▶ **Education Services Overview** – A one-day workshop that highlights each of the training opportunities described above.

▶ **Administrative Intervention** – In this workshop, a framework for handling office interventions is described, including how consistent discipline can be used to support teachers and help students successfully return to the classroom.

▶ **Reading is FAME®** – Four courses – Foundations of Reading, Adventures in Reading, Mastery of Meaning, and Explorations – comprise the curriculum of this adolescent reading program which has proven to dramatically improve the reading ability of students regardless of their existing skill level.

▶ **Common Sense Parenting®** – This program forges a partnership between teachers and parents, creating consistent expectations that are reinforced with children in the classroom and at home.

▶ **Specialized Classroom Management** – Training designed for special education environments, it outlines a proactive teaching approach that builds skills and self-confidence in students with emotional, behavioral, social, and academic needs.

BOYS TOWN USA®
Caring for America's Girls and Boys

For additional information
on how you or your organization can take advantage of these workshops or other partnership opportunities, contact Boys Town at the number below.
1-800-545-5771 or visit www.boystown.org

Book Credits

Production: Mary Steiner
Cover Design: Margie Brabec
Page Layout: Anne Hughes

48-007
9907-19-0004